YORK NC

General Editors: Pro
of Stirling) & Profe:
University of Beirut

C000185057

J. G. Farrell

THE SIEGE OF KRISHNAPUR

Notes by John Riddy

MA (OXFORD)
Senior Assistant Secretary,
University of Sterling

LONGMAN
YORK PRESS

YORK PRESS
Immeuble Esseily, Place Riad Solh, Beirut.

LONGMAN GROUP LIMITED
Longman House,
Burnt Mill,
Harlow,
Essex

© Librairie du Liban 1985

All rights reserved. No part of this publication may be reproduced, stored in a retrieval system, or transmitted in any form or by any means, electronic, mechanical, photocopying, recording, or otherwise, without the prior permission of the copyright owner.

First published 1985
ISBN 0 582 79288 6
Printed in Hong Kong by
Sing Cheong Printing Press Ltd

Contents

Part 1: Introduction   *page* 5

  Life of J.G. Farrell   5

  A note on the text   7

Part 2: Summaries   9

  A general summary   9

  Detailed summaries   13

Part 3: Commentary   48

  Themes and questions   48

  Historical background   49

  The characters in the novel   56

Part 4: Hints for study   59

  How to improve your understanding of

    The Siege of Krishnapur   59

  Extracts appropriate to particular topics   61

  Answering questions on the novel   62

  Plan for sample answers to questions   62

Part 5: Suggestions for further reading   69

The author of these notes   72

Part 1

Introduction

Life of J.G. Farrell

James Gordon Farrell, born in 1935, was only forty-four when in August 1979 he was drowned in the waters of Bantry Bay, in south-western Eire. He had apparently been fishing by the shore; a picnicking family saw an abnormally high wave sweep him out to sea. Partially disabled from the waist upwards by poliomyelitis, a wasting disease suffered when he was twenty-one, Farrell was not able to swim in the rough seas. His body was later washed ashore. He had settled in a farmhouse on Cork's Sheepshead Peninsula only four months earlier, having moved back to his beloved Ireland from London a relatively wealthy man, acclaimed and garlanded in his lifetime like few other contemporary writers.

Farrell had been born in Liverpool, but spent much of his childhood in Ireland. His parents, who both came of Irish stock, returned to Ireland after the second world war, leaving James at an English public school, Rossall, in Fleetwood, a fishing port on the coast of Lancashire and a terminus for the ferry service across the Irish Sea. The Irish connection seems always to have been strong. After leaving school, where his reputation seems to have depended largely on his enthusiasm for rugby football, Farrell taught for a while in Dublin, before going to work in the far north of Canada as a firefighter on the American early warning radar defence network (the DEW system). Up till then he had been mainly interested in sports, excelling in rugby football, enjoying cricket, and in the process building up—as we see from photographs of him in his late teens—a burly physique. Pursuing his craving for physical sports, he had broken his nose five times.

Nonetheless, his academic record at school was good enough for him to have secured admission at the age of twenty-one, in 1956, to Brasenose College, Oxford, to read law. His first few weeks at Oxford seem mainly to have been spent on the sports field. Indeed it was while he was playing in a rugby match, towards the end of his first term, that he was struck down by the early symptoms of 'infantile paralysis'—poliomyelitis ('polio')—which, when it is not fatal, is a disease which usually, even in our own times, leaves its victims more or less paralysed in some part of their bodies. In Farrell's case the disease left him with seriously damaged muscles from the waist upwards. According to his friend Malcolm Dean*, when Farrell recovered sufficiently to be able to emerge from the iron lung which had kept him alive during the crisis of his disease, it was found that 'his diaphragm no longer worked properly...his shoulders...and right arm were...restricted'. He had to learn anew the simplest human functions such as breathing. To cut meat had become a difficult gymnastic feat, as had even belching. His hair went permanently white during his illness. It is not perhaps fanciful to attribute to his own illness, and the long period of convalescence, that brooding interest in the symptoms and clinical history of the more serious diseases of man, and the slightly contemptuous descriptions of some medical practitioners, which occupy so much of *The Siege of Krishnapur*, and indeed of other works such as *The Hill Station*, also set in India.

Having, apparently as much by his own fierce will as by medical science, survived polio, Farrell returned to Oxford, but not to law. The nine months away from his studies could not be recovered: instead, needing a slightly gentler academic option, Farrell took the Final Honour School of Modern Languages, concentrating on French and Spanish in which he secured his Bachelor of Arts degree with third-class honours in 1960. He later taught English at schools in France, and began writing. His first novel, *A Man from Elsewhere*, which was published in 1963, was set in France, and took as its theme the conflict between communism and individuality.

In 1965 Farrell's terrible experiences with polio, and his memories of the ordeals he had had to surmount in order to rebuild his shattered body during the long convalescence, supplied the story for *The Lung*. The hero of *The Lung* is a Martin Sands, who is an aimless though apparently well-to-do drifter, a drunk, a divorcé, when we first meet him. However, deep down in his spirit Sands has considerable resources of pride and character waiting to be developed. It is perhaps not fanciful to see in Sands's career Farrell's own memories of his comfortable if aimless youth, before his illness, and his own responses to the challenges posed by the threat that he might always be a cripple. Sands finds the inspiration to show us human character in its braver, more generous aspect in the aftermath of polio. He is determined that, come what may, he will not be a vegetable. He will love—and make love. He will enjoy the normal pleasures of life—even drinking alcohol in spite of doctor's orders and problems with his own body's metabolic processes.

After publishing *The Lung*, Farrell was awarded a Harkness Fellowship which enabled him to travel, mainly in the United States. *A Girl in*

* 'A personal memoir' by Malcolm Dean, in the appendices to J.G. Farrell's unfinished novel *The Hill Station*, Fontana, 1982, p.193.

the Head, an imaginative experiment which many critics thought unsuccessful, concerning the strange life and absurd loves of one Count Boris Slattery, the last survivor of a great Polish noble family, followed in 1967.

In 1970 *Troubles* was published, restoring Farrell's reputation by winning the Geoffrey Faber Memorial Prize. Set in Southern Ireland shortly after the first world war, the novel is about Major Ripon, an Englishman back from the horrors of the war to renew an old romance in a setting dominated by a huge crumbling hotel, and by a society rent by civil war and violence that finally engulf the Major.

In 1971 Farrell travelled extensively in India, gathering material for his next book. In 1973 came *The Siege of Krishnapur*, and the winning of the Booker-McConnell prize; in 1978 there followed *The Singapore Grip*, and Farrell was engaged in the drafting of *The Hill Station* when he was drowned. Britain's Far Eastern empire seems to have attracted an ever-increasing share of Farrell's attention. *The Singapore Grip* is an ambitious story of the collapse of the defence of Singapore in 1942.

Always a solitary character, after his attack of polio Farrell seems to have become even more retiring. His tastes were for travel, old books, fine wines (he became an acknowledge connoisseur at Sotheby's wine sales) and good cooking. The few who were privileged to be close friends attest his warmth and wit when relaxed. To the outside world he seems a remote, elusive character.

A note on the text

The Siege of Krishnapur was first published by Weidenfeld and Nicolson, London, in 1973. This edition is now out of print. In 1975 it was published by Penguin Books, Harmondsworth and reprinted in 1979, twice in 1980 and in 1982. This commentary is based on the Penguin edition.

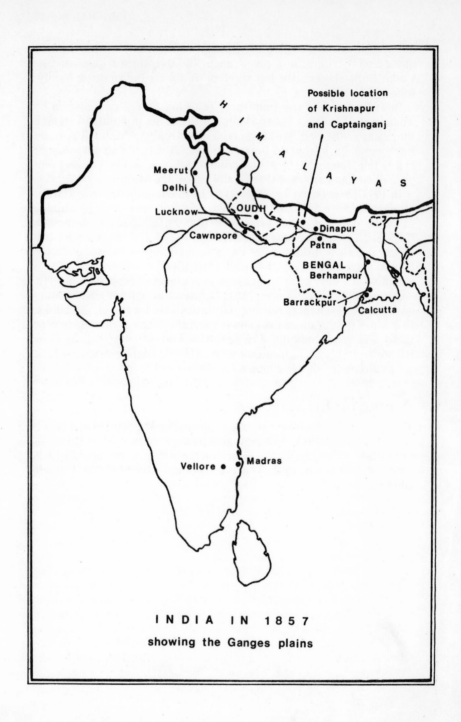

INDIA IN 1857

showing the Ganges plains

Part 2

Summaries
of THE SIEGE OF KRISHNAPUR

A general summary

The Siege of Krishnapur is set in India, in the year 1857. Almost all the action takes place in Calcutta, in those days the capital city of both the British Indian Empire and of the Bengal Presidency, and in Krishnapur, a fictitious town which might be some four hundred and fifty miles west of Calcutta, on the western border of what is now Bihar State. We only know that Meerut, sixty miles or so north of Delhi and the storm centre of the Indian sepoy mutiny that was to break out on 10 May 1857, is some five hundred miles to the west again. There is no other clear hint as to the Krishnapur location. There is a river, a mere trickle in the dry season, a vast torrent when the Himalayan snows melt, but it does not have a name. Similarly, there is a nearby cantonment or permanent military settlement called Captainganj, but it is impossible to find any place of that name in the great *Gazetteer of India*.

The events of British India in 1857 and the early months of the Sepoy War (or India's first War of Independence as Indian nationalist historians were to call it) are seen through the eyes of a small group of English and Scots men and women. Most are either employees of the Honourable East India Company, the dominant territorial power in the Indian subcontinent, or their dependents. There is Mr Hopkins, the Collector or chief administrative officer with great powers, civil, military and police, over the district around Krishnapur, a large man with bushy side whiskers who reminds other characters of a huge benign cat. When we first meet him, he is about to send his wife to England to recover from the loss of a baby son. He is a devout believer in scientific progress and the perfectibility of man. In his belief England has a mission in India to make possible the moral and material progress of the teeming millions there.

He has visited the Great Exhibition in 1851, and has not merely been reinforced in his faith in orderly progress by the exhibits he saw there, but he has brought many, both artistic and utilitarian, back to Krishnapur. Nonetheless, however imbued he is with the sense of natural, scientifically-ordered progress, he is also deeply worried by the signs of native unrest typified by the mysterious circulation of bundles of chapatis, the standard unleavened wheat bread of India. He has ordered the building of a massive rampart of earth round the Residency and other buildings of the headquarters of the British administration of Krishnapur.

Other characters whose experiences we share in some detail include Tom Willoughby, the Magistrate of Krishnapur, endowed with ginger hair and beard and an atheistical sardonic intellect; Dr Dunstaple, Krishnapur's medical officer, who represents medical obscurantism; Dr McNab, a gentle Scot who by contrast embodies all the intelligence and questioning genius that medicine can command, and who has recently been widowed. Dr Dunstaple's son Harry is a cheerful, out-going lieutenant in the Honourable East India Company's artillery, by luck and favouritism stationed at Captainganj very close to Krishnapur and his comely sister Louise. There is George Fleury, indolent, wealthy, conceited, the son of an East India Company Director. He has intellectual and poetic aspirations. George has recently come down from Oxford. He sees himself as a romantic, much given to the gratification of his senses, 'the victim of the beauty and sadness of the universe'. He is in many ways innocent and unworldly. However, sartorially he is very smart; his clothes are the envy of his less wealthy contemporaries. He has come to India to write a report for the Company's Directors on the progress being made by the natives of India, and to escort his sister Miriam Lang on a voyage which it is hoped will help her to forget the recent loss of her husband, the late Captain Lang, who had been killed in the Crimean War. Fleury has an introduction to Dr Dunstaple, who is an old friend of his father. It is an idiosyncrasy of Farrell's style that George Fleury is referred to almost without exception throughout the novel as 'Fleury', whereas his friend Lieutenant Harry Dunstaple is 'Harry' at all times. The Collector is rarely identified as 'Mr Hopkins'; usually he features as 'the Collector'. Farrell seems to find it difficult to decide how intimate we, the readers, are to become with the leading characters. Minor characters, depending partly on their social status, are identified apparently by the remote courtesies which would have been used by their social superiors at that time. There is 'Mr' Rayne, who is employ-ed by the East India Company as its Opium agent (a senior and most lucrative employment), and later during the siege, features as a black-marketeer. At a lower level there is Vokins, the Collector's English butler, whose only wish is to survive to die of old age in Soho (or wheresoever he has sprung from). But it is difficult not to be confused by the lack of consistency in the names of Farrell's characters; we are never quite certain how closely we are being invited to sympathise with, or to identify with, any one of the heroes. No sooner are we on first-name terms than abruptly, carelessly, we are required to return to the formality of the surname and so we are placed at arm's length just as our curiosity and sympathy begin to respond to the author's inventions.

Only Harry Dunstaple and his sister Louise, Fleury's sister Miriam Lang, and the unfortunately disgraced Lucy Hughes, remain with us on Christian-name terms; yet all these characters remain at a secondary level of identification in the obscurity of supporting roles, as they provide challenge, inspiration or counterpoint to the more seriously explored personalities of Fleury and the Collector.

It is also noteworthy that Indian natives hardly feature. It may be that Farrell did not feel confident enough about India and the Indian psychology to embark on any major investigation of an Indian personality exposed to the pressures and temptations of the troublous times. There is a vignette, the beginnings of an intimate sketch, of Hari, the Maharajah of Krishnapur's son. He is shown to have a keen interest in Western technological progress, and the scientific methods on which Western technological progress apparently rested; he is restrained under duress as an involuntary guest of the Collector in the Residency during the early days of the siege; but then, before we become too closely acquainted and, possibly, before the stress of exploring his Indianness becomes too burdensome for Farrell, he is allowed to slip away and disappear forever during a lull in the siege, as indeed do the Indian servants, the normally essential washerwomen, maidservants, cooks and bearers. We are left, for reasons of historic veracity, with the loyal Sikh sepoys digging saps and trenches and wells, but never intruding their personal idiosyncracies by so much as a phrase into a novel which finally has to be seen as a limited, even scanty exploration of Europeans under stress and deprivation.

The book is divided into four major parts and thirty-two chapters. The first part, with nine chapters, takes us from the first appearance of trouble in early 1857, with the ominous 'chapatis' being discovered in strange places, no one knows whence or why (save that the Collector recalls stories that a similar plague of unleavened bread preceded a great mutiny by the East India Company's Madras army at Vellore in 1806). This part continues past the final outbreak of general mutiny at Meerut, to the time when sleepy Krishnapur, far from the epicentre of the troubles, is itself engulfed by mutiny, the mass murder of Europeans, military and civil, adult and infant, and of Christian natives. As the section closes the sadly reduced European survivors, who have all been introduced to us against a background of gentler occasions, have retreated, along with a few loyal sepoys, mostly Sikhs, to the fortified encampment the Collector has prepared around the Residency. From the roof can be clearly seen the blazing houses and offices of the Europeans and of any Indian suspected of supporting or abetting the European or Christian cause. The blaze is 'like some mysterious sign isolating a contagion from the dark countryside' (Chapter 9).

Part Two, with eight chapters, takes the reader through the opening stages of the siege, and the first major attacks by the mutinous sepoys fresh from their successful revolt against their officers at Captainganj and their sacking of the European quarter at Krishnapur. The pages of this part are crowded with incident, as the European and Sikh defenders have to cope with siege conditions, the shortages of water, of provisions of all sorts, above all the total absence of privacy. Unfortunate clashes of personality abound. The Church of England padre reveals his abrasive and unintelligent nature, finding in every calamity justification for the good works of his Anglican God, quarrelling with the Roman Catholic priest over the division of scarce burial space for the dead of the two churches, and increasingly obsessed by his morbid awareness of man's sinfulness. Dr Dunstaple's professional antagonism towards his younger, more intelligent Scottish colleague Dr McNab comes clearly to the surface. Even in adversity, the ladies cannot find enough Christian charity in their conventional souls to forgive Lucy Hughes for her indiscretion in having allowed herself to be seduced by a young officer, and thus to lose that mysterious asset, her virtue. As Part Two closes, we are made increasingly aware of damage, both to the defences and the buildings within them and to the psychological constitution of the leading characters. Hunger, filth, disease, terror, all the squalor of a siege sustained without adequate resources, have reduced the noblest character, the Collector, to a condition wherein the shattered framework of his erstwhile Residency reflects the damage to his own mind. His faith in progress, in the scientific amelioration of the lot of man and in particular of the suffering millions of India, under the leadership of educated Western administrators like himself, is destroyed.

Part Three, with ten chapters, takes the reader through July and August 1857. The monsoon rains are slow to break. When they do come, they bring not relief but added misery. Every roof leaks; all the walls are pierced through and through by cannon shot, leaving the garrison, ever diminishing in number, exposed to the furious elements. The bodies of the dead rot, unburied, unconsumed by the overfed vultures, and the stench is appalling. Worse still, the rains begin to wash away the ramparts and, cruelly, cause the vegetation to grow and serve as cover for the mutineers' attacks. The Collector is afflicted with erysipelas, a dangerous condition that can lead to gangrene and death. He recovers, only to fall prey to a nervous breakdown brought on, it seems, by the unremitting burden of leadership, of keeping up morale, of preventing members of the garrison from quarrelling among themselves, of husbanding scanty resources, and, worst of all, of having to make every decision, great and small, on which survival may depend. During his absence the doctors' antipathies burst out in a virulent quarrel over the causes of and cure for cholera. Dr Dunstaple catches the disease and dies, rejecting to the last the efforts of Dr McNab to save him. The Collector recovers his nerve by a superhuman act of will and overthrows a black-market racket in dead men's foodstuffs organised by the odious Mr Rayne.

In Part Four, of five chapters, the rains cease and the mutineers mount a desperate assault. Mr Hopkins reduces the defensive perimeter to the last bastion, the banqueting hall. The few remaining defenders, including, luckily, all the main characters except Dr Dunstaple, prepare themselves for more assaults and the exhaustion of their last rounds of ammunition. They are ready to blow themselves up with the last of their gunpowder. In the nick of time, they are relieved.

Detailed summaries

Part One: Chapter 1

The opening scene is set in the apparently barren, endless plain of the Gangetic basin of North India in the long dry season. Mud-walled native villages can hardly be discerned through the glare of the fierce sunlight. The monotony of the vista is relieved first by the relics of some abandoned Muslim ghost city whose superior brick-built mosques have defied the ravages of climate and neglect; then by a deserted European cantonment or settlement, built in an earlier opulent era by the East India Company's servants.

At the end of February 1857 Mr Hopkins, the Collector of Krishnapur, is deeply disturbed by finding bundles of Indian unleavened bread 'chapatis' placed, it seems, intentionally in his way. He ponders on the vulnerability of the European population to a native uprising; he recalls that 'chapatis' had been baked and circulated throughout India as a signal before the mutiny at Vellore, fifty years before in 1806.

We are introduced to the Collector as a human being. He has served the East India Company for many years, indeed he is within a year of retirement. He is a man of considerable dignity, inclined to be moody and overbearing with his family. His wife, who has borne seven children, including a recent addition, a son, is unwell and is about to go back to Britain to recuperate.

As he meditates on the significance of the 'chapatis', and wonders whether the Residency, his official home and offices, and the immediate surrounds could be made defensible against attack, he is disturbed by the proceedings of the Krishnapur poetry society which are being held in a Residency room. Tom Willoughby, the magistrate, the other senior Company civil servant in Krishnapur, has been telling the wives and families of Krishnapur's Europeans, who have assembled to read their own poetry, about the merits of phrenology, a pseudo-scientific theory, popular in the mid-nineteenth century, according to which every human's mental characteristics can be discerned accurately by the shape of his or her cranium. Tom, whose wife, unable to bear the heat, has long since left India after a short spell of marriage, has a cynical turn of mind, and delights in devastating criticism of the ladies' poetic efforts. Once the Collector joins the group the discussion turns from phrenology to poetry: in spite of the Collector's efforts to restrain him, Tom is again brutally rude about the ladies' latest compositions. The Collector's wife and four daughters are in the room (only the two eldest children, boys at school in Britain, and the youngest, still a baby, cannot be present). The Collector is obsessed by vague fears inspired by the appearance of the 'chapatis'. Later, before he escorts his wife to Calcutta to catch the boat to England, he orders a rampart to be built round the Residency's grounds.

NOTES AND GLOSSARY:

mustard: a major non-food crop throughout India

frightful pond: a muddy, stagnant evil-smelling pool of water

Bricks are undoubtedly ... : by an ironic use of phraseology, Farrell pokes gentle fun at the average European's relief at again seeing buildings made of brick (rather than mud) betokening civilisation, comfort, company

domes and planes: the domes are clearly from the context the domes of mosques; equally clearly from the context the planes are not the trees of that name. Presumably Farrell means us to visualise the straight, architect-designed outlines of deserted mosques and tombs

Company: the English East India Company, the Honourable East India Company, John Company (Chapter 14), Company Bahadur (Chapter 31), to give it a few of its many impressive titles. The English East India Company was founded in December 1600, and by a series of first Royal, then Parliamentary Charters exercised a monopoly of the trade between the Indian and Pacific oceans and Britain. In the course of the seventeenth and eighteenth centuries, largely as a result of the collapse of the Moghul Empire in India and in order to protect its investments, the Company's servants, often without head office permission, took part in the civil wars which rent India. In course of time and after strenuous resistance from the French and the Dutch, who also had East India Companies with similarly ambitious servants, the English Company eliminated the European opposition and found itself with the powers of a kingmaker in India. In the name of the Moghul Emperor of Delhi, the Company exercised these powers to acquire direct territorial rule; its chief interest, apart from trade and access to India's mineral resources—especially diamonds and saltpetre—was to acquire control over the Land Revenue, that is the immemorial taxes on land paid by Indian farmers. It was the collection of the Land Revenue, the most important source of tribute India could offer, which led to the senior company servant in each district being known as Collector.

Such power and wealth created great enemies for the Company, both in India and in Britain. By the beginning of the nineteenth century the opposition, in Parliament and amongst non-Company trading communities, was so fierce that the Company had to compromise on its monopolies, in order to safeguard its final asset, its right to govern the Indian sub-continent. In 1813 it gave up its monopoly on direct trade between India and Britain, while retaining the lucrative monopoly on trade with China. In 1833 it renounced trade altogether except for the State monopoly on opium, which was produced and sold mainly to the Chinese and Malay markets (hence the role of Mr Rayne as the opium 'factory' manager). The Company retained the right, however, to pay its shareholders a dividend of 10%, about £720,000 per annum secured on the land revenues of India. After the mutiny, the Company lost its right to govern. Its assets, liabilities and servants were transferred by Parliament to the British Crown in 1858. Whether the Company's role in the evolution of India was more beneficial than harmful is a most fruitful subject of controversy among historians, and will doubtless remain so. Farrell's interpretation seems to be that the Company was weak because its servants in India were frail, inadequate and insensitive agents, spiritually bankrupt however wealthy in pocket they might have made themselves. Even the Collector himself, the most visionary and educated of the Company's representatives, has by the end of the book lost his faith in the justification of his presence in India as an improver and an introducer of higher, scientific Western civilisation

heaven knows what else: Farrell hints at the squalid excesses in taste, erotic pleasure and other gratifications that in former times had been within the means of the East India Company servants. Some readers may find this phrase lax

chapatis...biscuit: the usual North Indian chapati, unleavened bread, is rolled out as thin as the Indian housewife can manage, is soft (unlike a biscuit), and is designed to be rolled up so that small portions can be broken off to accompany each mouthful of the dish which it accompanies

*khansamah***:** steward of the Collector's household, the senior of the many domestic servants a Company civil servant might well have ·

Joint Magistrate: given that Tom Willoughby is about to be introduced as the Magistrate, the Joint Magistrate would have been the third most senior civil servant in the Krishnapur district

portico: an elaborate verandah with a high roof and columns, attached as a porch to the Residency building

palliate: literally 'to hide, cover as with cloak', the usual meaning is now 'to soften', 'to mitigate'

'Jilmils': Venetian shutters

ants: white ants, termites

Dr Gall of Vienna: along with a Dr Spurzheim the joint founder of the case for phrenology to be treated as a science

phrenology: the theory that every human mental and spiritual attribute is reflected in the development of certain surface areas of the brain, which in turn can be measured accurately by the shape (the 'lumps') of the surface of the skull

free-thinking turn of mind: a free-thinker is strictly one who refuses to submit his thoughts or theories to external authority, usually in religious matters. It is a term especially applied to those from a Christian background who wish to reject Christian orthodoxy or even to deny Christ altogether

in the celibate manner: because Tom's wife cannot stand the boredom of official life and the stunning heat of India, and has gone home to Britain, Tom lives alone

ginger hair: why Tom Willoughby's ginger hair should be taken by contemporaries as confirmation of his atheism is open to speculation

'civilians': the colloquial title given to members of the East India Company's senior civil—as distinct from military—service

an erl-king: in German Romantic poetry, the king of goblins (mischievous and ugly demons) reputed to live in the dark forests of Germany. The world of spirits, fairies, pixies and goblins was of great interest to Romantic poets from Johann Wolfgang von Goethe (1749–1832) to Sir Walter Scott (1771–1832) and Lord Alfred Tennyson (1809–92)

thickly armoured: means that the wall was covered with paintings, not that the paintings added any armour-plated reinforcement to the walls. This point is quite important in the light of events to come

plum cretonne: a purple-coloured fabric of great strength, made of hemp warp and linen weft threading. Cretonne is normally held to have been developed around 1870, later than the events in this novel

statuettes in electro-metal: figurines made of solid metal, usually a cheap base metal such as brass, but embellished with a coating of another usually much more valuable metal, usually silver or gold, by electrolysis. Thus was the appearance of value given to cheap artefacts, a notion of great appeal to the Victorian mind. The process was relatively new, having been described in scientific journals in the mid-1840s.

the Great Exhibition: held in a vast hall of cast-iron frame and glass built in Hyde Park in London, largely at the instigation of Prince Albert, the Prince Consort to Queen Victoria. The Exhibition was intended by implication to demonstrate Britain's engineering, manufacturing and scientific pre-eminence, and also, in part, Britain's financial and political stability in contrast to the instability and revolutionary fever that had bedevilled so much of the rest of Europe in the aftermath of 1848, the year of revolution.

The Exhibition was so popular that a great profit was made, even on the very low admission cost, which financed the purchase of a large site in Kensington, and the erection of the present buildings of the Imperial Science Museum. Again Prince Albert played a major part in both inspiration and execution. To Mr Hopkins, until the siege, it epitomised Western science and the triumph of Western civilisation

Edmund Burke: (1729–1797), of Anglo-Irish Protestant descent, was famous mainly as an eminent parliamentarian in the British House of Commons, and as a philosopher

enamoured of the rational: Tom Willoughby believes that human reason is the only worthwhile guide in matters of religion, and that no knowledge based on instinct rather than reason, is worth knowing

determinism: the notion that anything that happens, or that humans do, is determined by an inevitable chain of causation, which of course precludes the possibility that faith or repentance, can, on divine intercession, alter fate

Krishnapur Mutton Club and of the Ice Club: British society in Victorian India depended for the comforts of life on the willingness and ability of the Europeans to club together for the building and staffing of a place for recreation and reading (the 'Club' of immemorial usage), and also for the raising, protection, slaughter and butchery of sheep fattened to the European taste; and similarly for the building of deep cellars in which ice laboriously imported from North America, or more rarely the hills of India, would be preserved, a thankless and expensive task in the years before cheap electricity and refrigeration

the mutiny at Vellore: Vellore, a garrisoned town and cantonment some eighty miles west of Madras, in the deep south of India, presumably about a thousand miles from where Krishnapur might be surmised to be. In 1806, apparently as a result of rumours that both Muslim and Indian soldiers were about to be forcibly converted to Christianity—rumours fanned by the introduction of unfortunate military regulations about soldiers' dress, which succeeded in offending both Muslims and Brahman Hindus, and by misguided missionary zeal on the part of certain East India Company chaplains—the Indian native regiments stationed at Vellore broke out in mutiny. They killed some four hundred European soldiers from a European regiment garrisoned with them. The mutiny failed to gain support among other Indian regiments in the Company's service and was soon quelled with the usual ferocity

compound: the grounds and associated buildings (often very extensive) of any large house, usually enclosed by a stout wall, earthwork, or barbed wire, or prickly-pear fence

Chapter 2

The scene changes from Krishnapur to Calcutta, the gay completely Europeanised capital of British India. We are introduced to George Fleury, the son of Sir Herbert Fleury, formerly an East India Company official in India, now a director of the East India Company; and to Miriam Lang, George's sister, whose husband has recently been killed in the Crimean War. George has come out to write for the Company a book about the progress of India. We also meet Dr Dunstaple, the Civil Surgeon from Krishnapur, his wife and daughters, Louise and Fanny. Dr Dunstaple and Sir Herbert were at school together many years before, and still keep up correspondence. Sir Herbert has, from the patronage at his disposal, found a career in the East India Company's army for Dr Dunstaple's son Harry.

The Calcutta social season is in full swing. There are excursions to Barrackpur to picnic under the Great Banyan tree, balls and dinners. We come across Mr Hopkins, the Krishnapur Collector, now bidding his wife Caroline farewell. He is obsessed by his fear over the threatening implications of the circulation of 'chapatis' by Indian watchmen, and exposes himself to the ridicule of well-bred Calcutta as a result. Nonetheless there are other alarming portents. It is clear that the Indian native units of the Company's army are deeply disturbed by the fact that in loading a new type of muzzle-loader rifle currently being issued to all troops, it is necessary to bite the top off a pre-packaged weather-proofed cartridge containing both powder and shot, before ramming the load down the barrel of the new gun. Rumour has it that the cartridge that has to be bitten has been waxed with a tallow grease made from the mixed fats of the pig and the cow. Thus the sacred taboos of both major faiths, Muslim and Hindu, in the Company's Indian army, are deeply offended, and the biter is defiled.

Meanwhile George Fleury, who is a romantic young dreamer with scholarly pretensions, imagines himself enamoured of Louise Dunstaple, in spite of the many eager young beaux she already seems to have attracted. The rivalry is intense. Fleury is unathletic, even fat, and given to romantic dreaming, but he is very wealthy and his clothes are infinitely more fashionable than those of his rivals. Louise's mother, the powerful Mrs Dunstaple, approves.

NOTES AND GLOSSARY:

civil surgeon: the senior surgeon responsible for public health (as opposed to Dr McNab who is an army surgeon and whose responsibilities are confined to his military charges) and also by convention the personal doctor for all the senior European officials in the district.

As a matter of necessity the Company had been training Indian students to qualify as doctors through the Hindu College at Calcutta, since the early 1830s. Medicine was also about the only profession that a man of mixed blood (a 'Cranny', as Farrell calls such people in Chapter 8) could take up with some hope that in the end he might possibly cross the social divide and become acceptable in Indo-European Society. Hence the importance of the social mistake Fleury makes in assuming that Louise Dunstaple was born in Britain and must know the perils and horrors of the sea voyage out to India. Her fear is that as she has been born and brought up in India, Fleury might possibly believe that her mother may be a person of Indian or mixed blood, and that she herself might not be therefore socially acceptable as a wife for him

Lord Canning: Canning (1812–62) was Governor General and later first Viceroy of India, 1856–62. Often called 'Clemency' Canning because of his avowed policy of leniency towards the mutineers after the Mutiny

awarded a cadetship: one of the last perquisites left to the Directors of the East India Company, as the Company had divested itself of its trading monopolies by 1853, was the right to make appointments by direct patronage to all the positions of emolument under the Company. The Directors used their patronage not merely to oblige friends and relatives, but also to build up networks of political influence. The Civil Service appointments were thrown open to public competition in 1853; but the directors could still appoint to military commissions. Hence Harry Dunstaple's good luck

ortolans: in Anglo-Indian usage 'ortolan' means a lark, but the name was sometimes also applied to members of the bunting family. Quite why such small inoffensive birds should feature in an exchange of sporting anecdotes is a little mystifying

'Tweedside': tweed, a twilled woollen, woven material of coarse texture. It had been featured in the Great Exhibition as an example of textile innovation from the Scottish borders area, the Tweedside, and especially Galashiels. Normally, perhaps, an unsuitable cloth for the tropics

the Chowringee: the name of a road, and of an area inhabited by the smart, wealthy and in those days, usually European, merchant princes of Calcutta

whirring: presumably an allusion to the calls made by the nightjar, a nocturnal bird common in parts of Britain in the summer

gharry: (also often called *gari*, *garri*) a cart, a carriage. A *dakgharry* (mentioned in Chapter 3) had four wheels

Alipore: a suburb to the south of Calcutta

'But no native women': a taboo grew up, apparently in the early years of the nineteenth century, against any form of liaison between the transitory British (predominantly male) community and Indian women

verbena: a scent derived from vervain or other plants of the laurel family

'my youngest child, a boy, died just six months ago': but see Chapter 1: 'only the youngest . . . was excused'. There appears to be a discrepancy here, for the baby that is apparently alive in late February 1857 is held shortly afterwards to have died several months previously

daguerrotype: A photograph taken by a process invented by a Frenchman called Louis Daguerre (1789–1851), and described by him in 1839. The process (later demonstrated by Hari son of the Maharajah of Krishnapur) consists in sensitising a silver-coated metal plate (which has been exposed to light and to the subject of the photograph) with a solution of iodine; and then, after exposure of the plate to mercury fumes, a clear image of the subject emerges

crinoline: an underskirt made of a stiff material, a mixture of horsehair and cotton or linen, used to keep the skirts of dresses extended, away from the legs

country born: born in India, a condition carrying with it the unfortunate suspicion that one or other of one's parents had not been of pure British blood

ghat: in this context, a wharf, or river landing-stage

Dravidian: the name given by anthropologists and historians to the aboriginal peoples of India driven into the deep south by the Aryan invasions of India some four thousand years ago. Normally only applied to those Indians of deep brown or blackish hue and flat features who are to be met south of the Narbuda river. It is extremely unlikely that any Dravidians would be met in North India, round Calcutta. Presumably this misidentification springs from Fleury's ignorance of India

the Botanical Gardens: at Sibpur, on the west bank of the river Hooghly, just south of Calcutta

sais: (*Hindi*) a groom (in charge of horses)

Great Banyan: this tree, *Ficus Indica*, is a botanic wonder. As its branches spread, they put down roots for support and sustenance, and if left to itself the banyan can indeed spread over a great area. Records exist of one tree covering some three hundred acres. The buttress-like roots give the impression of a botanic cathedral. Hence Fleury's ecstasy

Moselle cup: a 'punch' or drink compounded of fruit, fruit juices and alcohol—in this case German Moselle wine

Enfield Rifles: long-barrelled guns designed to provide the Indian army with a weapon to replace the old 'Brown Bess' musket. This Enfield rifle was muzzle-loading, like the old musket, but the barrel was rifled (grooved spirally), giving the user the advantage of range and accuracy. The ammunition came pre-packaged in grease- and water-proofed paper containers (see the introduction to this chapter for the grave consequences of the use of this packaging)

maidan:	(*Hindi*) plain. A large expanse of grass at the centre of Calcutta
the Mofussil:	the provinces, as opposed to Bombay, Calcutta, Madras, the Company Presidency towns (from an Urdu word of Arabic origin meaning 'separate')
Opium and Salt	revenues: opium and salt were a government monopoly in British India, and a major source of income. Indians were forbidden to make their own salt from the brine by the seashore (See Barlow, a man from the Salt Agency in Chapter 7)
card:	at formal balls it was the custom for the order of the dances to be printed on small cards, which were issued to the ladies. It was then possible for eligible men to seek the privilege of one dance or more; if approved, the dance would be allocated to him on the lady's card. To have an empty card just before a ball commenced was the ultimate misery for a girl
'nautch':	Hindi word for a dance (display). It was most unusual for nautch girls to dance with anyone untrained for the classical dance patterns of India. Nautch girls were notoriously also prostitutes
General Hearsey:	a real-life hero (1793–1865) of the events, much as painted by Farrell. The episode must therefore be dated after 29 March 1857, when the gallant act took place on which Hearsey's fame as the first hero of the Mutiny rests

Chapter 3

We accompany George Fleury and his sister Miriam on the last stages of their journey up from Calcutta by postal coach (or *dak gharry*). Harry Dunstaple has come to meet them. They arrive in Krishnapur just when, unknown to them, the Indian Mutiny breaks out at Meerut, five hundred miles away. There is a dinner party at the Collector's Residency, with much talk of the nature of progress and civilisation, in the light of the Great Exhibition. Nonetheless, Fleury finds this society dull. Next day he accepts an invitation to take tea with Mr Rayne, the Opium Factory manager, at whose house the mood is one of careless frivolity and unrestrained self-indulgence by the young bloods of the Civil Service and the British army.

NOTES AND GLOSSARY:

dak gharry:	Hindi words rendered phonetically. A four-wheeled, rapid and light carriage used for carrying mail and officials of the Indian Government

nabob:	corruption of the Urdu *Nawa'b*; applied to the rich European merchants of the East India Company
betel:	it is a widespread and, to foreign visitors, alarming custom throughout India for persons of both sexes to chew the leaf of the betel tree (*Piper betel*). Coated with areca-nut, chopped and mixed with lime, it is eaten as a postprandial stomach-settler. This chewing paste gives the lips and teeth a vivid and blood-red tint
gorse:	prickly bush of extreme toughness found in temperate climates
fool:	from an Urdu word, meaning 'fruit'; a delicate dish of cream, sugar and sieved fruits, in this case mangoes
Tractarian:	name given to the ideas of those Church of England, mainly Oxford-based, clergymen who wrote the ninety 'Tracts for the Times' 1833–41. This in turn led to the Anglo-Catholic revival and the conversion of many Anglicans to Roman Catholicism in the 1840s and 1850s
dak bungalow:	a self-catering hostel, built for senior government servants (into which category all Europeans regardless of rank were deemed to fall)
punkah-wallah:	in the days before electric fans and air-conditioning, the unhappy wretch who spent his whole day agitating a large fan suspended from the ceiling
Sahib:	(*Hindi*) term of respect for one's social superior
Lord Bhairava:	a Hindu deity. Bhairava is a manifestation, in terrible form, of Siva, the great force of creation and destruction. Bhairava is portrayed in many different forms, mostly with three eyes, and up to ten arms; he is usually associated with relatively modern developments of Hindu sectarianism, based on the Tantras, writings of religious and ritualistic instruction

Chapter 4

The signs of Indian unrest become clearer. The Collector, the one man able to foresee events, is sleepless with worry. He consults, in the absence of Dr Dunstaple, the senior doctor at Krishnapur, the wise young Dr McNab. They discuss the precautions that Mr Hopkins is trying to take against political unrest. Mr Hopkins is not wholly certain that he is doing the right thing, building large trenches round the

Residency, trying to accumulate stocks of food and ammunition in anticipation of a siege. McNab notices that Mr Hopkins's daughters (for whom the Collector now has sole responsibility in the absence of his wife in England) are overdressed and obviously in great fear of their father: they even have to read him their diaries.

Reports of arson from the Indian regimental quarters coincide with the arrival of General Jackson, the elderly Military Commander of the nearby cantonment of Captainganj, who refuses to believe that there is anything sinister in any apparent signs of unrest. He despises Mr Hopkins for taking precautions, claiming that these very precautions will cause precisely that anxiety and unrest among the natives that the Collector finds so alarming. The Collector, aware of the terrifying responsibility resting on his shoulders, and of the possibility that, being human, he may be mistaken, tries to impress the world with his confidence by forcing his wretched daughters to play croquet with him under the scorching sun.

NOTES AND GLOSSARY:

ayah:	a children's nursemaid or nanny
havildar:	an Indian officer
lines:	the neat rows of military dormitories, and of commissioned and non-commissioned officers' houses in a British army cantonment (permanent military camp). The same town plan was followed all over India
sepoys:	(from Hindi *sipahi*) Indian soldiers
insouciance:	heedlessness
croquet:	a game played by knocking balls with hammers through hoops. It can cause bad temper

Chapter 5

In this chapter George Fleury and Harry Dunstaple go to visit the Maharajah of Krishnapur (who turns out to be abed, asleep, so the visitors are entertained by Hari, the Maharajah's son); while Miriam Lang and Mr Hopkins go to visit the nearby opium factory.

Harry Dunstaple is taken ill upon arrival at the Maharajah's palace. Hari looks after George, showing him the Maharajah's collections of weapons, dirty pictures and bric-à-brac. Hari takes an elaborate daguerrotype portrait of George, but the embryonic friendship between the two wilts as George unwittingly insults Hari's ancestors and possessions. Miriam is entertained at the opium factory by Mr Rayne's asssistant, Mr Simmons; and on her way home, is finally bored to sleep by Mr Hopkins's speech on the benefits which Western civilisation can bring to India.

NOTES AND GLOSSARY:

zemindars: Indians with the power—and the duty—to pay the government taxes on a given area (from Persian *zemin*, land); loosely, landowners

landau: an open, sprung four-wheeled carriage

pericardium: the membrane that surrounds the heart

Zouaves: local troops levied to help the French to fight their early nineteenth-century wars in north Africa. They were celebrated for the exotic shapes and colouring of their uniforms, and for their ferocity in battle

Blackwood's Magazine': a monthly magazine, published by the Scottish firm of Blackwoods in Edinburgh, containing fictional and factual accounts of adventures with an Empire background, much esteemed in India and the colonies

dhoti: loincloth, traditional Indian male attire. The typical garb worn by Mahatma Ghandi after taking over the leadership of the Indian National Congress

'Namaste': Indian greeting

durzie: tailor

godowns: warehouses

God Kartikeya: a Hindu god. Like Bhairava's his distinguishing feature is a multiplicity of limbs

pater: (*Latin*) father

Morpheus: Roman god of sleep

cow: to the Hindu, the cow and all its products are holy

ryot: peasant-farmer, who in this case would have contracted to grow opium poppies as a more rewarding cash crop than, say, mustard or sugar-cane

Chapter 6

In this chapter we learn that the storm clouds of mutiny have reached Captainganj. Mr Willoughby, the magistrate, has been on his rounds, trying to cajole Hindu landowners, *zemindars*, to build up the river embankment to prevent seasonal flooding of low-lying lands. The landowners prefer to sacrifice black goats to propitiate the river gods. They console themselves for the magistrate's tongue-lashing by repeating rumours of massacres of Europeans at Captainganj. Willoughby himself does not yet know of the rumours, which surface abruptly while he is complaining to the Collector about the recalcitrant landowners, as the badly wounded General Jackson is brought into the Residency by a few loyal sepoys.

Meanwhile, Fleury, recovering from the noxious gases released by Hari's daguerrotype picture-making, and, freeing himself from the metal clamps, eventually finds Harry Dunstaple and they make their way home from the Maharajah's palace, unmolested even though unarmed.

NOTES AND GLOSSARY:

ghat:	here, in this context, it means a flight of steps leading down to a sacred river (which might be the Ganges). Some steps permit the devout Hindu to descend to bathe; at others the dead could be burned so that their ashes might be cast into the sacred river
Brahmins:	the highest, sacred caste among the Hindus, divided into a large number of sub-castes
Sircar:	the government, that is, the British Government in India
feringhees:	(originally Persian) Franks, Europeans; used pejoratively by 1857 to mean any insensitive, ignorant white man
sowars:	soldiers mounted on horseback

Chapter 7

In the first panic after the massacre of Europeans at Captainganj, the whole of the Indian and British Christian community flocks to the Residency for safety, bringing all their worldly goods with them. The Collector tries to establish order out of chaos, organising the defences. The centrepiece of Mr Hopkins's fortification is the banqueting hall, surmounted by gigantic busts of Greek philosophers. Mr Hopkins insists on using the church for storage of food and military equipment, much to the chagrin of the Padre who also finds ample matter for controversy in the allocation of burial space (for all the likely fatalities) to the Roman Catholic community. The Collector orders the destruction of a mosque overlooking the Residency's defences; his conscience is troubled at the expediency of this action, sacrilegious to all Muslims.

Fleury and Harry Dunstaple are sent to try to induce the unfortunate seduced Lucy Hughes to leave the remote and dangerous *dak* bungalow and come into the safety of the Residency. Neither has any experience of coping with the emotional problems of women. They fail in their mission.

NOTES AND GLOSSARY:

indigo: staple commercial crop of northern India, down to the first world war and the German discovery of synthetic blue dyes. Indigo is a plant requiring careful tending and processing if it is to produce the rich, vivid blue-green dyestuff for which it was famous, and esteemed by the textile industry. The supervision of indigo planting and cropping was usually in European hands

hackeries: light bullock-drawn carts

Sikhs: the followers of the tenets of the ten Sikh saints, mainly compiled into the Sikh Sacred Book: the *Adi Granth Sahib*. Sikhism is a faith which originally aimed at reconciling Hinduism and Islam. Proscribed by both Hindu and Muslim authorities, and after much persecution by the Moghuls, especially in the early eighteenth century, Sikhism became a major religious force in the Punjab. The Sikhs and the British had clashed in two major wars in the 1840s, whereafter the Sikhs became one of the favourite, and mostly loyal, recruiting sources for the British Indian army. By and large the Sikhs stood by the British throughout the terrors of the Mutiny, with great courage. They were truly the unsung heroes of Lucknow, and Delhi, and indeed Krishnapur

Salt Agency: the production and sale of salt throughout British India was a government monopoly, the penalties for infringing which were extremely severe. Mahatma Ghandi drew attention to the absurdity and harshness of the monopoly in 1931 by leading a march of Congress workers to the sea to take up the saline efflorescence

Dinapur: the military cantonment of Patna, which was presumably not far from Krishnapur

chase: the firing end of a cannon's barrel. The cascable is the handle at the gun's breech-end

futwah: the pronouncement on any point of Islamic law or morals by a Muslim law officer attached to the British courts of India

Chapter 8

There is a temporary lull in the action. The mutineers at Captainganj being undecided about whether to march off directly to Delhi, to pledge allegiance to the last, nominal, legitimate Moghul ruler, Bahadur Shah the Second, or whether to attack the Krishnapur Residency, the latter is left in peace. The Collector tries, without great success, to keep the normal administrative processes going. Within the Residency no one is under any illusion; all, and especially the ladies, manoeuvre to make their life as pleasant as possible, if need be at other people's expense.

Fearing that supplies will not suffice for a siege if too many are given sanctuary, the Collector reluctantly drives Indian Christians out to fare as best they can, armed only with certificates of good conduct.

General Jackson dies, the first European casualty in the Residency. The Padre, thinking the time opportune to recall his European flock to the ways of God, is dismayed at the poor attendance at his sermons. He sees the cause of the present calamities in the sinfulness of the European character.

Harry Dunstaple and George Fleury renew their attempts to persuade Lucy Hughes to leave the *dak* bungalow and come to the Residency. They find her increasingly attractive. They still fail as Lucy fears the bitter tongues of her virtuous female peers.

NOTES AND GLOSSARY:

lâtees:	clubs
'Crannies':	from a Hindi word meaning 'of mixed caste'; Eurasian. Also often used of junior white recruits to the Company's civil service. The more usual word for people of mixed race was *cheechee*
Excalibur:	the sword owned by the legendary King Arthur, leader of the Knights of the Round Table
Bacon and Milton:	Francis Bacon (1561–1626), English philosopher and writer; John Milton (1608–74), English poet and pamphleteer, author of *Paradise Lost*
chignon:	a lady's hairstyle, with the hair swept up into a bun
gup:	prattle, rumour

Chapter 9

The interlude, following the Captainganj massacre, continues. The Padre, at a Sunday school for the children living in the Residency, attempts to prove God's existence from the evidence of the marvels of the creation of the world. Fleury challenges him, and they both quarrel. The Padre issues eagerly sought-for sweetmeats to the children; but the children are bidden to take these sweets to the Indian native Christians still sitting outside the Residency gates. The sweets are rejected by the Indian Christians, who fear to lose caste by touching tainted European products.

The mutiny's effects spread. Lucy Hughes finally comes into the Residency, reassured by Louise Dunstaple's offer of friendship.

As reports of spreading mayhem flood in, the Collector is again found dining amongst the manufactured miracles of his time, electro-plated imitations of the great masterpieces of sculpture and handicraft. His conscience is troubled as he has taken advantage of a visit by Hari to the Residency (to obtain a certificate of good conduct) to incarcerate him, and his henchman, the Prime Minister, as hostages to keep the Maharajah and his army from joining the mutineers.

NOTES AND GLOSSARY:

the Atonement: the Christian doctrine according to which Christ is held to atone for man's sins through his crucifixion

Moloch: pagan god mentioned in the Old Testament (II Kings 23:10)

a very dear friend of mine: Fleury's friend is evidently the poet Matthew Arnold (1822–88), who became a school inspector after attending Oxford University

Benvenuto Cellini: a famous Italian goldsmith (1500–71)

Part Two: Chapter 10

It is dawn on the day of the first direct attack by the mutineers on the Residency defences. The Padre, obsessed by the sense of sinfulness of his European parishioners, and by the clear manifestation of God's judgement in the impending destruction of the Residency and its occupants, is poor consolation to the frightened defenders as he goes round reminding everyone of their wickedness, and handing out Christian tracts.

Harry Dunstaple and Fleury have spent the night in anticipation of the attack, polishing and preparing a six-pounder cannon, and reinforcing their defences by pulling down busts of the Greek philosophers from the roof of the banqueting hall. As it becomes light, the mutineers open fire. A chance shrapnel shell kills most of the six-pounder gun team, leaving only Fleury, Harry and Ram, a faithful Indian retainer. Their appeals for reinforcement are fruitless. They can see large numbers of mutineers massing for the attack. They fire their six-pounder with desperate zeal. Fleury is impressed with Harry's scientific expertise with the large gun, and realises that he has been foolish to despise Harry for his apparent lack of social skills.

Nonetheless, Fleury, in a daze, finds it hard to concentrate on the present action.

NOTES AND GLOSSARY:

hydra-headed: the Lernaean Hydra of Greek mythology was a many-headed water-serpent. When one of its heads was cut off, two or three more would grow in its place

pariah dogs: filthy, unkempt, scavenging offspring of domestic dogs

portfire stick: a rod wrapped round with a rag dipped in pitch or tar, used to ignite cannon

the Redan at Sebastopol: allusion to an attack during the Crimean War (1854−6) on an outpost of the Russian fortress at Sebastopol. As the Redan was heavily defended, and the attack by the British infantry was not preceded by an effective bombardment, losses had been high

canister or grape: 'canister shot consists of lead balls loosely packed into cylindrical tin canisters' (Chapter 12); grapeshot is small bullets linked together

Plato and Socrates: Plato (c.427−c.347 BC) and Socrates (c.469−399BC), who was his mentor, are among the founders of Western European and Islamic philosophy

Coleridge ... Keats ... Lamartine: Samuel Taylor Coleridge (1772−1834), English poet and philosopher; John Keats (1795−1821), English poet; Alphonse de Lamartine (1790−1869), French poet and politician

trunnions: the mount on an old cannon carriage on which the cannon barrel swivelled up and down

limber: a detachable cart designed to carry shot and powder for cannon

Chapter 11

The opening of the siege worries the Collector. He realises he should have had levelled the native mud huts around the Residency, in which the mutinous Sepoys are taking cover. He tries to keep up his own and everyone else's morale by appearing in elegant garb, sporting a pink rose. But he is distraught and in his anxiety finds his thoughts caught by the sight of all the pets that the inmates of the residency have brought with them, sheltering in the shadow of the church. He remembers with affection a long-dead pet dog. He realises too late that he should have forbidden people to bring their pets with them. After inspecting the Cutcherry defences, where already the first to be wounded have fallen, he goes back to his study for a restorative brandy, his rose wilted. A musket ball, fired throught the window, ricochets around the study. The Collector dives to the floor in panic. He collects himself, determined to be a good example to the other besieged.

NOTES AND GLOSSARY:

pith helmet: a hat padded with compressed vegetable fibres to insulate the head against the sun's rays
RIP: (*Latin* 'Requiescat in pace') Rest In Peace
khet: (*Hindi*) field

Chapter 12

Harry Dunstaple has to instruct his tiny military unit in the rudiments of musketry. The Padre, intent on demonstrating to George Fleury the proof of God's existence from the perfected design of all creatures, interrupts. His examples are not all happily chosen: he believes that Indian hogs have yard-long teeth in their upper jaws with which to hook their heads over tree branches thus enabling them to sleep whilst standing up.

At the height of the Padre's nonsense, the long-threatened charge of the sepoys takes place. The defenders, even the Padre, the man of God, help to man the cannon, which destroys almost all the enemy cavalry and infantry. Nonetheless a few native cavalry avoid the deadly canister shot and for a moment both Fleury's and Harry's lives hang in the balance. Saved more by luck than skill, Fleury and Harry find the Padre still intent on proving God's existence from the perfection of His designs as manifest in man's works.

NOTES AND GLOSSARY:

firelocks: muskets
Sodom and Gomorrah: two cities destroyed by God (see the Bible, Genesis 19) because of the corruption of their inhabitants
frays its diurnal passage: goes on its daily journey
viviparous: bearing live young (compare *oviparous*, egg-laying)
heft: lift
'We gat not this by our own sword': from the Bible, Psalm 44:3

Chapter 13

It is 12 June and the siege has already been in progress for some days. The Collector, still the leader of the besieged community, goes on a tour of inspection. First he visits the billiard room which has been converted into a dormitory for ladies. The shortage of water, and the absence of servants, means that the ladies cannot look after themselves properly. Their quarters are cramped and dirty, and the smell is terrible. However, the Collector is disturbed sexually by the company of so many young women. He hands out a small present of flour, jam and suet with which the ladies can make puddings.

After a brief discussion with Tom Willoughby and Fleury on the ingratitude of the Indians in rejecting Britain's superior culture, the Collector goes to visit the improvised hospital in the stables, where Dr Dunstaple is conducting a passionate personal feud of startling animosity with Dr McNab, because of the latter's adoption of novel methods of practising medicine and surgery. Again the filth and the smells of a military hospital are overwhelmingly nauseating. Cholera has been confirmed. Almost all the wounds become gangrenous. The Collector is dismayed that Dr Dunstaple's animosity against McNab is near the point of insanity.

NOTES AND GLOSSARY:

dal:	a very thick lentil soup, a staple dish in India
Commissariat:	that part of a military organisation which is charged with responsibility for finding and paying for supplies of foodstuffs
cravat:	a kind of neck-tie
charpoys:	bed-frames
dhobi:	washerman
khus-tatties:	screens made of sweet grass
stays and spine-pads:	items of female underwear designed to enhance the curvaceousness of the figure
roly-poly pudding:	a kind of suet pudding made with jam
rock bun:	a small, heavy cake made with currants
Miss Nightingale:	Florence Nightingale (1820–1910), from her experiences in the Crimean War the founder of modern nursing and commentator on matters of public health
Permanent Settlement:	an act of 1793 by which the amount of land tax to be paid on any given tract of land was to be fixed for all time, regardless of fluctuations in yield or in the price of the produce of the land
woad:	blue dye

Haileybury or Addiscombe: Haileybury was the training college for the East India Company's civil servants, Addiscombe for its military cadets

Congreve rocket: a crude missile, the forerunner of the modern rocket

bhoosa: dry straw

Chapter 14

We see a further stage in the siege mainly through the Collector's eyes. He regrets that by permitting the butchery of the captive sheep from the Mutton Club, in the wrong place, by the croquet court, he has condemned the besieged to a horrific miasma. Even the vultures and jackals are no use: they have so much dead meat to gorge on elsewhere that they no longer can be relied on to clear the debris of death near the manned areas.

He checks the work of the few soldiers in the garrison who are competent at mining engineering, building listening tunnels to frustrate the sepoys' efforts to sap (undermine) the defences. He remembers from his military reading that, in theory at least, the cause of his sickly, reduced garrison is lost. But he knows that the one option he cannot take is to surrender.

He wonders what to do about the relics of those who have died. To sell, to the advantage of the rich: or to divide, equally among equal sufferers. He cannot make up his mind.

Mr Hopkins's rounds are enlivened by the smells of fresh food cooking in the encampment, overlooking the Residency, of the crowds of eager Indian onlookers for whom the horrors of the siege are simply entertainment. Mr Hopkins no longer finds the presence of the onlookers humiliating.

He calls on Hari, now housed in an old tiger house alongside the hospital. It has been noticed that the sepoys do not shell Hari's quarters. Usually Hari and Mr Hopkins exchange bitter words; Hari craves release, but today is anxious to discuss the phrenological science he has been studying.

Mr Hopkins helps the Padre to dig graves. He weeps but composes himself lest he cause the garrison to lose heart, on seeing his tears. Later, taking tea with young officers, he impresses everyone by his refusal to take cover when musket balls begin to fly. Only he himself notices that his hands shake so badly he cannot put sugar in his tea.

NOTES AND GLOSSARY:

olfactory: pertaining to the sense of smell

orange flowers: Farrell's not very apposite metaphor for the flashes of shot

Vauban:	Sébastien de Vauban (1633–1707) was one of Louis XIV of France's generals, whose fame rests on his theories about defensive systems
Place assiégée, place prise:	(*French*) a position besieged is a position taken: a favourite phrase of Vauban
saps:	tunnels, intended to enable gunpowder to be placed under the enemy's lines
thugs:	ritual assassins who killed travellers in the name of the Hindu goddess Kali by strangling them with a scarf known as the *rúmal*
F. Rabelais:	François Rabelais (c1494–1553), French satirist, author of *Gargantua* and *Pantagruel*
J. Swift:	Jonathan Swift (1667–1745), Anglo-Irish satirist, author of *Gulliver's Travels*
'Man that is born of woman . . .':	from the Bible, Job 14:1–2
Caesarean section:	method of childbirth used when natural delivery is impossible, whereby an incision is made in the mother's abdomen
gastrotomy:	stomach surgery
pubes:	genitalia

Chapter 15

It is 7 July 1857. A mine prepared by Lieutenant Cutter at the end of a tunnel dug under enemy lines is finally ready to be exploded. Fleury prepares to take part in a charge of the few horse-mounted men left, to take advantage of the enemy's shock. He has invented and had made—how, we are not told—a fiendish new weapon, part pitch-fork, part crook, with which to 'eradicate' enemy horsemen.

The mine is sprung. It has a devastating effect. The enemy is too dazed to resist. The small cavalry charge is fairly successful, although Fleury's new weapon reveals problems of design and is rejected. A friend is killed. The enemy's cannon are either captured or spiked.

NOTES AND GLOSSARY:

Carnot:	a French general (1753–1823) of the Revolutionary period
howitzer:	a cannon designed to drop shells from a great height

Chapter 16

Fleury, returning in triumph as a brave hero from the horse charge, finds that his friends have prepared a small birthday party for him with a few pathetic luxuries. He is the darling of all the women: Miriam, his

sister, is relieved to discovered that he is not a coward, and Louise
Dunstaple begins to find him attractive (albeit she seems to be preoccupied with incipient boils, the result of inadequate diet and dirt).
Louise is also chagrined that her brother Harry finds Lucy Hughes, the
dishonoured woman, so clearly attractive. All the women have com-
bined to fashion a present for George Fleury. With the Collector's
permission they have cut up the cloth on a billiard table and made
George a coat of green cloth.

NOTES AND GLOSSARY:

Cupid: Cupid, Roman god of love, is traditionally held to
                     shoot arrows which cause those wounded by them
                     to fall in love

Diamond Head: signal-station at the entrance to the River Hooghly

Sherwood Forest: associated with Robin Hood, who according to
                     tradition wore Lincoln green (like Fleury). Robin
                     Hood is a mysterious figure of English folklore,
                     who is presumed to have flourished at the end of
                     the twelfth century. In most legends Robin is
                     depicted as a brave, ingenious nobleman, outlawed
                     unjustly by the villainous Regent, John, ruling
                     England during the absence of King Richard I
                     (Richard Coeur de Lion) on Crusade against the
                     Saracen, and later, in the prisons of the Christian
                     Emperor of the Romans in Germany. Robin Hood
                     is said to have robbed the rich and tyrannical in
                     order to help the poor and the needy, hiding, when
                     pursued, in the thickets of the then great Forest of
                     Sherwood, near Nottingham. The historic reality
                     and the true achievements of Robin Hood are both
                     subjects of some controversy among professional
                     historians

Chapter 17

It is still 7 July 1857. Mr Hampton, the Padre, obsessed with the sinfulness of his flock, attributes God's wrath and the perils of the siege to
George Fleury's refusal to believe in the Atonement. He longs to
exorcise the devil in Fleury. As he digs graves for the latest fatalities, he
prays that Fleury may cross his path so that debate can be reopened.

The Padre is helped by the Collector, who in his turn is increasingly
preoccupied with the clear sense that the success of the British depends
on his example and his morale. Father O'Hara and the Padre quarrel
over the identity of dead bodies wrapped in their sacks. Fleury finally

does arrive, to help dig graves. Mr Hampton immediately engages him in close theological argument, holding to the literal interpretation of the Bible. Fleury, on the other hand, still euphoric in the afterglow of his birthday party, puts up a feeble case for the Bible to be seen as a set of moral truths rather than a constricting assemblage of literal truths.

The Collector meanwhile, bored by this theological discussion, revises yet again his plans for the defence of the compound in view of the rapidly dwindling number of men able to bear arms and the scant supply of powder and shot, and very conscious of the fact that time is running out.

NOTES AND GLOSSARY:

Thirty-nine Articles: the essential doctrines of the Church of England
Coleridge: presumably the poet Samuel Taylor Coleridge
Machiavelli: Niccolo Machiavelli (1469–1527), Italian political philosopher
velocipede: early form of bicycle, with the cranks on the front wheel

---

Part Three: Chapter 18

By Chapter 18, the first chapter of Part Three of *The Siege of Krishnapur*, the Collector is feeling the strain. Worse, he is beginning to suffer from the erysipelas that will shortly force him to an invalid bed. Dr McNab notices, but makes no comment. Mr Hopkins releases Hari from house arrest.

The river is swollen with melting snows from the far-off Himalayas, but the rains do not come. Death is all around. Fleury is upset by the death from sunstroke of a young girl. Lieutenant Cutter has been killed: Dr Dunstaple breaks down under the stress of unremitting toil in the hospital and retires to his bed for a day or two. When he returns, his rancour against Dr McNab, who has looked after his wards in his absence, redoubles.

NOTES AND GLOSSARY:

Himalayas: a range of high mountains defining the northern boundary of India
chaplets: wreaths, garlands
General Wheeler at Cawnpore: General Sir Hugh Wheeler (1789–1857), after a siege somewhat like that of Krishnapur, surrendered in June 1857. The survivors, men women and children, were all slaughtered with two chance exceptions. The last leader of the Mahrattas, Nana Sahib, is usually held responsible for the massacre

Chapter 19

The time has come for the implementation of Collector Hopkins's plan for the withdrawal of the diminished numbers of the garrison from the Cutcherry and Dr Dunstaple's house. The Cutcherry has been the record store for the district. The architect of the plan, Mr Hopkins, is now suffering acutely from erysipelas. He tries to watch the withdrawal through his telescope, but can hardly bear the pain of the eyepiece. His agony is redoubled when be accident he focuses on the Cutcherry just as it is blown up to prevent it being used by the enemy. The pain of the blinding flash reduces him to delirium. He notices the distant onlookers cheering. To his disturbed mind, the cheers bring ease. The Indian natives are happy, and so British rule is justified.

The enemy attack, sensing victory, but are driven back by artillery fire and by a snowstorm of old documents from the demolished Cutcherry, which blinds and bewilders the charge at the moment of victory. The magistrate orders the scattered documents to be collected up from the ground, but the task is soon abandoned.

Fleury, smarting from his intellectual defeat in the graveyard by the Padre, reads through his Bible (which he carries as body armour) for passages in which crime and violence seem to be glorified, the better to confront the Padre, a literalist believer in the divine truth of every word in the Bible.

NOTES AND GLOSSARY:
tamarind: a shade-giving tree, common in India

Chapter 20

His erysipelas has finally caused Mr Hopkins to collapse. Fleury finds him prostrate, and in his ignorance and alarm imagines the affliction to be cholera. Dr McNab gently disabuses him, and involves Miriam Lang in the task of nursing the Collector. Louise Dunstaple, although she is a doctor's daughter, is momentarily shocked at the problems of coping with the natural functions of a sick man's bed, but rallies after a moment's thought. She is more concerned at the moral danger in which Lucy Hughes has put her brother; Miriam points out that in the crowded conditions they all live in there is little likelihood of a consummation of the relationship. Louise muses on the possibility of marriage to Fleury.

The rains at long last begin to fall, and in great abundance.

NOTES AND GLOSSARY:
aperient: a laxative, any medicament to keep the bowels
                       open

alimentary canal: the bowels
erysipelas: a feverish condition of the body marked by skin rashes of great extent and painfulness
laudanum: an alcoholic extract of tincture of opium, used as a sedative
bearers: the universal term in India for general servants hired to perform unskilled household chores. Remarkable in this context in that it shows that even at this late stage in the siege there were still Indian servants who were prepared to suffer with their British employers rather than take the easy option of running away
'And everywhere he is in chains': from the opening sentence of *Le Contrat Social* by the French philosopher Jean Jacques Rousseau (1712–78): 'Man is born free and everywhere he is in chains'
Eheu, fugaces: a Latin tag expressing regret at the swift passage of time. It is not surprising that Louise does not know how to pronounce it, since Victorian girls were not taught Latin and Greek like their brothers

Chapter 21

Dr McNab is worried that Mr Hopkins's erysipelas is getting worse, and that blood poisoning may be setting in. He varies the treatment.

The rains have brought a lull to the battle. The humidity causes the unburied dead to fester and rot; the smells hanging over the beleaguered garrison are even more evil than they have been, as there are no winds to carry the stench away.

Relief seems increasingly illusory. Men begin to lose faith in God and, in Mr Hopkins's case, in the belief that India's natives were happy to be introduced to the benefits of Western science and civilisation. Mr Hopkins slowly recovers. Though feeble, he tries to resume his work. He fails.

NOTES AND GLOSSARY:
pyaemia: blood poisoning
bark: quinine (ground bark of the cinchona tree)
chloric aether: chloroform dissolved in alcohol
miasma: a fetid gas

Chapter 22

With the setting in of the rains, a new plague in the form of enormous clouds of winged beetles arrives nightly, attracted by the fires and candles. Lucy Hughes tries to hold a tea party, but just as it is about to start in fly columns of the beetles. As luck will have it they settle on poor Lucy. She is hysterical with repugnance and fear, and tears her clothes off in her frenzy to rid herself of the insects, but in vain. She faints, covered with mounds of insects. Her friends Fleury and Harry Dunstaple set to, to scrape the insects off her body. Never having seen a mature woman's body before, they are amazed and perplexed at what they discover. Other friends including the Padre come in, and are in their different ways shocked at what they see.

NOTES AND GLOSSARY:

cockchafers, 'flying bugs': the cockchafer is a beetle, which on emerging from the chrysalis swarms in enormous quantities. The normal swarming time is May, but it can happen later. H. Hobbs, in his memoirs of life in Bengal in the 1880s called *It Was Thus* (Calcutta, Thacker Spink, 1918, p.77), recalls that on one occasion the swarms attracted to the candle lights of certain Calcutta hotels were so enormous that bullock carts had to be hired to carry away the mounds of dead insect corpses

'gothic': carved in a pseudo-medieval style

***Andromeda Exposed to the Monster*:** In Greek legend, Andromeda was bound naked to a rock, to be devoured by a sea-monster. She was rescued by Perseus

Chapter 23

It is early August. Hope Mary Ellen Wright has just been born to a newly widowed mother in the besieged Residency, and is to be baptised by Mr Hampton. The garrison, seeing in the ceremony a symbol of possible survival against all odds, gathers to witness the baptism. The Collector, who is to be godfather, muses on recent developments. He is pleased in a small way that he has learned to wash his own clothes, acquiring the art from the native *dhobi* who has remained with the garrison. The Collector's example has caused everyone else to try to wash their own clothes; the *dhobi*, angered, has fled from the Residency. Other sanitary problems have arisen, as genteel folk have found lice in their hair and clothes, and Mr Hopkins has had to use all his authority to get people to help one another to comb out their hair. He ponders on the frailty of women, and concludes that it arises as much from their lack of education as from their nature. He remembers the grotesque end of the pious Mr Bradley, who, mortally wounded, dies in the arms of the atheistical Mr Willoughby. The Collector no longer finds his Christian faith a very certain source of comfort.

NOTES AND GLOSSARY:

Madonna:	the mother of Christ
Saint Peter:	in Christian tradition, the gate-keeper of heaven

Chapter 24

The monsoon rains continue to fall heavily. Lucy, recovered from the episode of the cockchafers, is having another tea party, at which a prize guest is Mr Willoughby. It is not that Mr Willoughby finds Lucy sexually attractive; but as a phrenologist he is interested to verify her cranial bump of 'amativeness'. He wonders how he can secure the opportunity of feeling her head without being misunderstood.

Meanwhile the Hindu *zemindars* gather to sacrifice a black goat to prevent the rain-swollen river overflowing onto their lands. The sacrifice appears to work.

One other, more disastrous effect of the rains has been the erosion of the earthen defences of the Residency. The Collector, in spite of universal protest, orders the dissolving battlements to be protected by the Residency furniture, including possessions brought in by the refugees. Everything is sacrificed to try to preserve the defences.

Harry Dunstaple has a scheme for cutting down the rank vegetation that now covers the sepoys' advances with chain shot fired from the cannon; but how can he make such shot? The Collector solves the problem by producing a special file bought at the Great Exhibition. The Collector now rejects his own earlier enthusiasm at the material progress the Exhibition has symbolised for him. Harry asks when he should begin firing the chain shot. Tired of having to make every decision, great or small, the Collector says: 'Please yourself', much to everyone's amazement, and then, even more shockingly, retreats to his bed although it is mid-day.

NOTES AND GLOSSARY:

sal **trees:**	trees planted for shade, like the tamarind
Amativeness:	propensity to love
haemophilia:	(here used metaphorically) an unstanchable flow of blood
tumbrils:	carts carrying coffins, or the bodies of the dead, to which 'the possessions' are likened
humidors:	containers, by means of which a level of moisture can be preserved in a dry climate
eights:	rowing teams consisting of eight oarsmen and a coxswain
chain shot:	cannon balls chained together to create a deadly missile capable of cutting a broad swathe through ranks of men or vegetation

Chapter 25

In spite of the Collector's withdrawal to bed, where he stays for days without speaking to anyone, the defence continues. One evening after service in the cellar beneath the Residency the latent animosity between Drs Dunstaple and McNab breaks out in open controversy over the cause and treatment of cholera. Dr McNab, who does not claim that he himself, or medical science, has yet solved the problems, appears to lose the debate to the furious Dr Dunstaple, who is wedded to traditional notions which the intelligent, sceptical Magistrate, Mr Willoughby, senses are ignorant and unscientific.

NOTES AND GLOSSARY:

Nunc Dimittis: (*Latin*) 'You now dismiss'. The first two words of a prayer based on Simeon's plea on seeing the infant Jesus: 'Now let your servant depart in peace', from the Bible, Luke 2:29

morbific: tending to produce a diseased condition in a living body

Newton: Sir Isaac Newton (1642–1727), English physicist, discoverer of the laws of gravity

Faraday: Michael Faraday (1791–1867), English discoverer of electrical induction

Bengal Club Cup or the Planters' Handicap: both are horse races

ganglionic nerves: a tumorous development in a healthy main nerve from which smaller nerves radiate

calomel: chloride of mercury

infusoria: a mass of small unicellular animals living together

Chapter 26

As the Collector is slow to recover from his collapse of will, the Magistrate, Mr Willoughby, as the next most senior officer, has taken over the command and has ordered the sale of the stores, including foodstuffs, of those who have recently died. The Collector who has been quietly regaining his confidence and working himself back to fitness by shovelling at the rain-threatened ramparts, attends the sale. He discovers that the bidding has been rigged by the still fat and sleek Mr Rayne, who is in charge of the garrison stores. The Collector dismisses Rayne and confiscates the stores of food of all the dead for general consumption, to general applause.

The sale suspended, the bidders to their surprise have to listen to the re-opened debate over the source of cholera between Dr Dunstaple, who is certain that the disease stems from an airborne taint, and Dr

McNab who is certain that it is waterborne. Dr McNab cites examples of tainted town water supply and of the working conditions of miners which seem to establish his case. At the height of the debate there is an enemy attack and everyone has to return to the ramparts. Dr Dunstaple in his chagrin, drinks an odourless, clear fluid from a bottle which, it is feared, might be the bowel discharge from a cholera victim.

NOTES AND GLOSSARY:

1832:	the year of the British Parliament's First Reform Act, which gave the vote to all male householders
Chartism:	a movement among the British working classes to establish certain rights defined in a six-point charter; largely discredited after 1848
factory reform:	the reform of inhuman working conditions in factories in Britain and India, usually associated with the moral leadership of Lord Shaftesbury (1801−85)
cerebral:	relating to the brain

Chapter 27

It is now August and the rains are almost over. Stocks of foodstuffs, of shot, and powder, are desperately low in the Residency. To make matters worse Dr Dunstaple comes down with cholera. He swears that it was brought on by the water he had drunk during his recent display of temper at the auction of foodstuffs. He gives elaborate instructions about his nursing, but rapidly gets worse. Dr McNab is called in, and injects a solution of salt and water to prevent the dehydration that he, McNab, sees as the fatal consequences of cholera. Dunstaple recovers, but is furious that he has been treated by McNab. He relapses after ordering the abandonment of the McNab treatment. Again McNab is called in, and Dunstaple recovers. Again the latter's anger causes the treatment to be changed. Dunstaple dies of a heart attack. People cannot make up their minds whether he or McNab was right.

Meanwhile George Fleury, having seen his beautiful pet spaniel Chloë eat the face of a newly-killed sepoy mutineer, orders his dog to be shot.

Part Four: Chapter 28

At the end of August, with the end of the monsoon rains, the spectators on the hill overlooking the Residency reassemble for the spectacle. By now the whole garrison, men, women and children, are near starvation; many are also suffering from scurvy. They can think of nothing else but food, and avidly watch the spectators cooking their sumptuous meals on the hillsides. Anything which can be digested is eaten: even disgusting pariah dogs and stray horses are caught and eaten. Children have to allay their pangs by chewing leather.

NOTES AND GLOSSARY:

chapatis, nan and parathas: different kinds of Indian bread

scurvy: a condition of the body due to the absence of vitamin C derived from fresh fruit and vegetables; common among those suffering from an inadequate diet, as on a long sea voyage or during a siege

Chapter 29

It is 12 September 1857, and the mutineers are massing for a great assault on the obviously weakened Residency. The Padre, Mr Hampton, is preaching one last sermon in the Residency's great hall, for the Collector has determined that on the next day everyone will finally withdraw to the banqueting hall for a last stand. Should that fail —and the Collector repeats for the umpteenth time his feeble encouragement, that he knows a relieving force to be on its way—then the last of the powder will be used to blow up the banqueting hall and everyone in it, to save the survivors from torture and dishonour.

Suicide being preferable to the dishonour of final defeat by the mutineers' assault, the Collector checks his firearms. The pistols and revolvers he had bought at the Great Exhibition are among the few really useful souvenirs remaining to him, all the other items having long since been consigned to shore up the ramparts. He catches a large beetle, which (after offering it to Mr Willoughby) he eats, being so hungry.

NOTES AND GLOSSARY:

gentlemen now abed: the Magistrate alludes ironically to the famous speech made by Henry V to his men before the battle of Agincourt in Shakespeare's *Henry V*, IV.3.64

David and Goliath . . . Israel triumphing . . . Daniel in the den of lions: the Padre refers to various Old Testament stories which, because they tell of victories over apparently hopeless odds, are intended to offer comfort

Archbishop Leighton: a Scottish churchman (1611–84), Principal of the University in Edinburgh in 1653, became Bishop of Dunblane, tried to preserve what was best in Episcopacy and Presbytery, but only succeeded in being misunderstood by both sides; he became Archbishop of Glasgow in 1669

Woolwich: a Thames-side suburb of south London where a major arsenal and military training school for artillery men were situated; new weapons were often tested at its shooting ranges

Chapter 30

It is 13 September; the day of the mutineers' assault starts with the beautiful sounds of someone singing in praise of a Hindu divinity. The assault begins; in spite of heavy losses, the mutineers press home their attacks and the garrison has begun its planned retreat to the banqueting hall.

Fleury is so absorbed by the intricate mechanisms of a pistol that has refused to fire that he almost stays too late in the Residency. At last, at the point where he is about to be killed by a sepoy, the pistol does indeed fire.

The Collector has planned a withdrawal from the Residency, room by room. The fighting is desperate, hand to hand; losses are heavy on both sides. It looks as though the Collector is finally lost, but he is saved by Harry Dunstaple, who manages to get his worn-out cannon to fire, as a dangerous experiment and at extremely long range, a red-hot cannon ball into the mutineers' magazine. The resultant explosion and blast cause the mutineers to pause long enough for the Collector to make his escape to the banqueting hall.

NOTES AND GLOSSARY:

Mogul emperors: a dynasty of Muslim rulers in India, tracing their descent from Timur the Lame and Genghiz Khan

muezzin: the Muslim priest who calls to prayer

'Spike the guns!':   to spike a cannon means to hammer a nail or similar object into the touch-hole, making it impossible to ignite the charge

Oudh: Uttar Pradesh in north India, the traditional recruiting ground for the Bengal army up to the Mutiny

subadar: the most senior military rank to which an Indian in the British military service could aspire; equivalent to a major

patchouli: a perfume derived from certain Indian plants

morbid: usually means 'diseased'; Farrell seems to intend 'deadly' or 'death-dealing'

the French wars: the wars between England and France (1793–1815) that followed the French Revolution

Sebastopol: a Russian fortress in the Crimea, the object of a long siege by the British during the Crimean War

Boney: a contemptuous name for Napoleon Bonaparte (1769–1821), who died more than thirty years earlier, but against whom these old gentlemen had fought in their youth

Chapter 31

It is 17 September. The number of Indian spectators on the hill has surprisingly diminished. Can it be relief at last? With no food left, and almost everyone in a coma through malnutrition, with only two days' expenditure of powder in store, and the only ammunition the filed-down remnants of the late Father O'Hara's crucifixes, of Mr Hopkins's electro-metal figurines, and stones, the garrison is reduced to the most miserable straits. Only the Padre has the energy for controversy, anxious now to establish, before it is too late, that the Great Exhibition was simply the triumph of Mammon, of materialism unrelieved by compassion. Mr Hopkins, whose memories of the Exhibition increasingly concentrate on the inhuman, including chains made in Birmingham for the slave trade, agrees. But suddenly there is a spell of excitement: the relieving force arrives, shocked at the state—especially the horrid stink—of the survivors.

NOTES AND GLOSSARY:

Jesuits: members of the Society of Jesus, an order of priests of the Roman Catholic church

thanes: lords

gutta-percha: a gum produced by a Sumatran tree, widely used in making special mouldings

Saint Sebastian: in Christian tradition, an early martyr who was put to death by being shot at with arrows

Beelzebub ... Baal ... Mammon: names of pagan gods mentioned in the Old Testament and in later tradition associated with the devil; here they stand for crude worldliness and materialism

'pandies':   a vulgar generic term for all the mutineers. One of the first known mutineers bore the Brahmin caste name of Pandé

untouchables: members of the lowest rank of humanity in (or rather, strictly speaking, outside) the Hindu socio-religious structure. The touch, and even the shadow, of these unfortunate people was held to contaminate any member of the four higher orders of Hindu society

sherry pawnee: a drink of sherry mixed with water; (*pani* = water)

Chapter 32

Once the Residency has been relieved, the Collector goes home, taking
with him as his last memory the sight of Indian peasants with their
bullocks at the immemorial task of drawing water in leather buckets
from a village well. His retirement is not glorious. He speaks little,
spends most of his time at his club, eating and reading the newspapers.
His belief in progress and good works has gone.

One day he happens to meet Fleury, who has married Louise
Dunstaple (but is now nonetheless on his way to an assignation with
another woman). Mr Hopkins learns that Harry Dunstaple has
married Lucy Hughes, and has become a general. Miriam Lang is
married again, to Dr McNab, the one man of whom, in retrospect, Mr
Hopkins approves. There is a short, indecisive conversation about the
value of ideas; and the two men part, Fleury to his self-indulgent,
trivial round, Mr Hopkins to his scepticism.

Part 3

Commentary

Themes and questions

One difficulty that you may have when reading *The Siege of Krishnapur* is that the author presupposes that you know more than a little about the context, about India, especially in the nineteenth century. Farrell also assumes that you know about the role of the British rulers of India, employees of a trading company, and their relationship, never simple, with the complex structure of peoples, traditions and religious taboos that made up, and still to a great extent makes up, the society of the Indian sub-continent. Furthermore, the novel is about the fragility of the moral and economic justifications for British rule in India. You, the reader, are meant to be able to discern the seeds of the decay of British rule in the characters and the events depicted in the story of the siege.

Farrell is in effect asking his readers certain questions: why, if the British were apparently so vastly outnumbered by the native races of India, were they nonetheless in control of this huge country? Why, if so many of them were so experienced in the ways of India—and Mr Hopkins and Mr Willoughby may be taken as models of their kind—were the British in India apparently so blind to the clear signs of impending danger? What fears made it impossible for Mr Hopkins to consider surrender to the mutineers? Why, with the military odds so heavily in their favour, did the overwhelming numbers of the sepoys not annihilate the Europeans? What were the passions, what was the background that suddenly caused one of the largest standing armies on the face of the globe, the largest after the Russian, and the German, to rise in simultaneous rebellion, apparently synchronised throughout the country? Was the conspiracy furthered through the circulation of unleavened loaves of chapatis that we first hear about in Mr Hopkins's despatch box (Chapter 1)?

The Siege of Krishnapur clearly aims to establish itself as a historical novel and to give you the answers to some at least of these questions. The title, it may be assumed, was intended to remind the potential reader of the fact that the novel is set geographically in India; and, historically, that the main development of the plot is set against the background of what historians, depending on their race and political outlook, have variously called the Sepoy Mutiny, the Indian Mutiny,

The Great Indian Rebellion or India's first War of Independence.

Equally, from an early moment in the novel we are made to see that for Farrell the interest lies in placing Mr Hopkins, as a creature very much of his time, and all the beliefs he held so dear, under stress. Mr Hopkins's commitment, seen at its clearest in his dinner speech (Chapter 3), is to the superiority of British over Indian culture; to the supremacy of the civilisation offered by British mercantile and mechanical prowess to the benighted peoples of the world; to the inevitable triumph of Western science and of ordered, statistically-informed Western government and administration over all the problems India might pose; and finally, to the existence of his God, as manifest through the apparent omnipotence of his faithful British servants; all these beliefs are to be tested by adversity and, we sense at an early moment, are all to be found wanting. But the context is everything, and the full poignancy of the final surrender of Mr Hopkins's beliefs can only be understood after consideration of the background both of those beliefs, and of the cataclysm that engulfs them in 1857.

Historical background

By the time that the story opens, the British had been in India for two hundred and fifty years, and British rule was to survive for another ninety years. For the first hundred and fifty years of their presence in India, the role the British played was that of merchants capitalising on a monopoly, granted by the British crown and confirmed by parliament, which the English East India Company, based in London, enjoyed over trade between Great Britain and the Far East. Territorially, in India, as elsewhere in the Far East, the interest of those merchants lay in their concessions, their trading posts and trade warehouses, the so-called 'factories' established with the permission of and on terms set by the local rulers. In India, trade concessions had mainly been granted by the Moghul Emperors, Muslims of remote Turkish descent who since the mid-sixteenth century had ruled over Central Asia and North and Central India, from Eastern Persia and Bokhara to Assam and down to the southern Deccan. The modern city of Hyderabad marked the most southerly extent of the vast territories that were directly subordinate to the Moghul Emperor. For concessions in the lands to the south of the Moghul rule, the English East India Company relied on pacts with smaller and more ephemeral ruling dynasties, which might or might not be adept at survival. And herein lay the germs of empire and tragedy. Following models established by European predecessors, the Portuguese, the Dutch, the French, and to defend themselves against the vagaries of local dynastic politics, the Company's agents believed it to be necessary to fortify their factories, their trade stores and emporia, with—or occasionally without—the permission of the territorial overlord. Fortifications need to be manned; and the Company recruited soldiers locally and in Europe. Once the Company employed small armies, naturally there was a standing temptation to take sides in local politics, which in the manner of the time and place, were often matters of small-scale armed conflict, and in which the disciplined, trained bands of the English East India Company could participate with profit. By the mid-eighteenth century the leasing of these small, but ever-growing armies had become more profitable, more immediately and fabulously lucrative for the East India Company than straightforward trading. Moreover, these armies certainly appeared to guarantee a social and political stability, and a respect for the Company's law and agents throughout India, without which trade withered and died. The taste for action, for territorial supremacy, grew. With the contemporaneous collapse of the might of the Moghul Emperors, reduced to puppet status by Persian and Afghan invaders and by the Mahratta rebellion, there was by the end of the eighteenth century no Indian power able to withstand the British. The French, the Dutch and the Portuguese had contested supremacy, for the same reasons as those that had motivated the British visitors. But the sea lanes were too long and the maritime resources inadequate for French or Dutch or Portuguese opposition to have been more than a significant irritant. Suddenly, from the welter of conflict the British arose clear and proud as the paramount power, the sole arbiter in India. The only Indian native states to survive were those prepared to accept subordination and allegiance to the company. Indian rulers might still be rich like the Maharajah of Krishnapur, but they were bereft of responsibility and spent their lives in idle self-indulgence or in the absurd amassing of trinkets, or, like the Moghul Emperors, they were reduced to the status of retainers, surviving until 1858 in narrow confinement and with the squalid trappings of such subsidies and rents as the British deigned to release. Meanwhile the British ruled—in theory, at least—as the white eminence behind the throne, and in the name of the Moghul Emperors. But to the Indians the rule of the East India Company remained rule by tradesmen, and no Indian forgot that if only in name the Moghul Emperor survived at Delhi, a last pathetic incarnation of Indian power, independence and grandeur.

To police the vast territorial empire they had acquired, the British needed to recruit a legion of educated administrators, like Mr Hopkins, the Collector, or Mr Willoughby, the Magistrate, to rule and to exploit the great sources of wealth, the Land Tax, and the proceeds of the monopoly staples of India. To give force to the decisions of these administrators, the Company recruited and paid a huge standing army. The East India Company paid the Government of Great Britain (whose involvement, through Acts of Parliament renewing the Company's monopoly, remained discreet) for royal regiments to serve in India; in addition the Company was allowed to recruit and train its own European regiments. Most important of all, the Company used its great territorial revenues, derived in the main from the Indian Land Taxes paid by the *zemindars* we meet sacrificing black goats to protect their dykes, and from the monopolies it enforced within India on the manufacture and sale of salt, and the manufacture and sale, in the main to China, of opium, to recruit three separate armies. These armies were based on the trading centres of Bengal, Bombay and Madras.

The Company trained large numbers of Indian regiments of these armies in the European style, officered by Europeans such as General Jackson and Lieutenant Dunstaple. The recruits came from the so-called 'martial races' of India and were called 'sepoys' or soldiers. For the Bengal army they came from the Brahmins and the Muslim families of Oudh (the modern Uttar Pradesh). So long as their pay was regular and their religious sentiments were respected, the myriad regiments of Indian soldiers in the East India Company's employ were loyal, and excellent fighting men. It must be stressed that there was nothing random about the Company's military recruitment. It was a clear policy, a policy which had paid dividends, to recruit for the Bengal Army from the high castes, and thus to ensure employment for educated and influential classes. The danger was that the Brahmins (high caste Hindus), tightly bound by ritual, and by clear and fiercely enforced religious observances and taboos; and the Muslims, descendants of Afghan and Turkish families which had for centuries served the Moghul Emperors and which still clung to their memories of the period when the Moghuls ruled India as Dar-ul-Islam, a land where Allah could be openly worshipped and where the Muslim law predominated, were all committed to extremes of religious observance and orthodox purity. It was a commonplace of high British administrative theory that India, and the vast hordes of the sepoy army, were to be treated like sleeping giants and that no policy was to be formed with might alarm the religious susceptibilities of the sepoys. But the Company, to justify its rule, was committed to improvement, and improvement meant change. There was also the problem that practice at the district level in India was somewhat different from theory in London or even in high places in Calcutta, the seat of the British administration in India.

Military triumph, success, power, wealth had all come so readily, so consistently over the years of the Industrial Revolution in England and Scotland, and of the French Revolutionary and Napoleonic wars—the period immediately preceding the time in which this novel is set—that many educated Britons saw divine sanction in the very extent of British power and wealth. The British thought they were God's appointed vassals. Padre Hampton cannot understand (Chapter 3) why the Bible was not originally written in English, as it was God's will to use English as His medium for bringing the Gospels to the heathen world! The notion of a manifest racial, religious destiny can be seen in minds of both Mr Hopkins and of Mr Hampton, the Padre. 'The spreading of the Gospel on the one hand, the spreading of the railways, on the other': here in Mr Hopkins's words (Chapter 3) are the twin missions for the British in India. The role that God has given to the British, they believed, was to uplift the peoples of India (and of course of other equally 'benighted' areas) and to bring them to a better social order, a more productive society based on imported Western techniques and manufactured wares, and of course on the message of the Christian Gospels openly or covertly incorporated into the acts of the administration and the legislation by which men defined right and wrong. The East India Company's Directors in far-off London might forbid Company servants to attempt to convert the Indian soldiers, but nothing—and we see this clearly in Mr Hampton's messages to his flock—could or should prevent Christian gentlemen and ladies from setting individual examples which in effect meant that outward behaviour, and one's every accountable action, should be seen by the world to be aggressively Christian. The Christian model of a correct life was by the mid-1850s not a matter for discretion and the inner conscience, but had become a matter for·unashamed open display, by men shaping what they felt was a new 'correct' system of society, often based on a literal application of the Gospels.

The reshaping of India from the apparently medieval squalor of Moghul times to the hygienic disciplined 'happiness' of nineteenth-century progressive modernity, was the responsibility of the relatively small band of British administrators, military officers and Christian (mainly Anglican) law-givers, and the Padres who guided their consciences, in whose hands lay total, almost arbitrary, power and authority. When individuals endowed with vast powers without accountability believe that their appointed task is to bring the benighted to reason, accidents can happen. The British community maintained, in outward aspect at least, a very narrow, conformist, consistently Christian posture, clearly and increasingly contemptuous of the teaching, traditions and practices of both Hindus and Muslims, and clearly and increasingly believing in British racial superiority over all other peoples. It would have been hard for even sympathetic, well-paid and humanely treated Indians not to fear that the spate of innovation, of radical change in the law systems, the social and administrative structure of India, in the methods of transport and communication, of commerce and industry, must all be leading to, or preparing the ground for, other, more sinister changes, in the religion of India.

It was the very pace of the changes the East India Company was introducing, often with clearly benevolent motives, to improve the lot of the Indians, that made the Indians fearful and the Company's British servants careless. The fear-filled taboos and inhibitions of Muslim and Hindu were seen as ignorant and unnecessary constraints on the dynamic machine of the improving state. Furthermore, it was assumed by British administrators like Mr Hopkins and Mr Willoughby that Indians, were, like their own womenfolk, by their nature backward, ignorant, fearful of necessary social and material change. Left to themselves, they would protect their lands from flood by sacrificing black goats rather than by building scientific dykes. Therefore when changes were introduced they were imposed from above, without consultation or explanation, speedily, with insensitivity. In the circumstances the wonder is that Indian hostility to the British had not vented itself in passionate, angry rebellion at an earlier moment. The only logical explanation for the delay in the outburst of Indian grievance must lie in the diversity of, and mutual antipathy between, so many of the tribes, castes and religious denominations of India. Although Muslim and Hindu had learned to co-exist, the relationship between the two great religions had been marked by so many violent outbursts of intolerance and persecution that co-operation between the two communities was incredible to the British mind. The British had profited from, indeed in the frame-work of the army, had sought to preserve, the divisions between the communities. Farrell draws our attention to the rivalry between Muslim and Hindu in the episode in Chapter 6, wherein Mr Willoughby returning from his abortive attempt to get the Hindu *zemindars*, or landowners, to build dykes, is diverted by the Muslim manservant making anti-Hindu jokes.

And yet the two communities did come together, in a brief alliance that was to prove tragical for them and for the British, who had inspired their terror, and become the object of their passionate outburst of hatred. It took the combination of a belief in the sudden fallibility of the British, and of imminent mass conversion to Christianity, to put the spark in the power magazine of the sepoy army. In the Crimean War, it was rumoured, British losses had been so huge that there were few white soldiers left to succour the garrisons of India, which in their turn had clearly been run down (whether as a matter of false economy or to provide reinforcements for the Crimea was a matter for debate). The sepoys' memories of service during the Afghan wars of 1839–41 and of the Sikh wars of the mid-1840s carried a vivid impression of how fallible the British could be, especially in leadership and military technique. The white regiments, and white officers, had lost the aura of infallible grace which had sustained them in earlier times. In a discontented India, rumour played a major role in increasing the general unease and creating the impression in both the army and the civilian population of incomprehensible change and of the arbitrary exercise of irresponsible power by alien white men who cared nothing for the Indian peoples over whom they exercised such great authority. In the months before the Mutiny there were several cases of British regimental officers, in defiance of custom and their orders, attempting to convert Hindu Brahmin soldiers to Christianity.

Suddenly, into this agitated world, there came the latest innovation of Western technology, a new main firearm for the infantry soldier, a rifled muzzle-loader which for speed of loading required pre-packaged powder and shot. The use of the new weapon is described by Farrell in Chapter 2 of the novel, as is the reason why the new weapon was supposed to bring with it a deadly contamination. No amount of earnest briefing and reassurance would convince the sepoy that the grease, essential for the effective insertion of the bullet, was not a tallow made of a compound of pork and beef fat (Muslims do not eat pork, which they regard as unclean; Hindus do not eat beef, because to them the cow is sacred). In fact once the military authorities had carried out the most searching examination of the processes that were used by the contractors, it was discovered that the anxieties of the sepoys did indeed have a sound foundation. By the time the investigation was completed, however, the damage had been done, and the whole of North India was ablaze. Almost every regiment of sepoys recruited in Oudh rebelled. Some mutinied enthusiastically; some rebelled with the greatest reluctance, and only after it had become apparent that in British eyes all sepoy regiments recruited in Oudh were, without further investigation, to be treated as treacherous rebels, and if military force was available, to be crushed, and massacred regardless of truth or justice or Christian forgiveness.

The Mutiny was conducted with terrifying brutality on both sides. On the sepoy side, it is clear, there were skilful manipulators of human tragedy who were prepared to go to any extreme of brutality in order, possibly, to compromise reluctant fellows and to make impossible any reconciliation with the British. Women and children were murdered along with soldiers and civil administrators, the armed and the defenceless alike. Prisoners were slaughtered without compassion, and in the worst incident of all, the British garrison was massacred in June 1857 following their surrender at Kanpur (the Cawnpore of so many Victorian historians). (In Chapter 18 we read of the rumours of this atrocity reaching Mr Hopkins and his garrison.)

Equally the retribution exacted by the British was often merciless in the extreme, and the punishments imposed by the authorities once

British power had been restored were not always informed by evidence, fairness or decency. In the chaos that prevailed in 1857–8 no one can tell how many human casualties were caused by the Mutiny. Certainly the losses on both sides, by murder or open battle, ran into tens of thousands. Cities were devastated. Delhi, the beautiful city of the Moghul Emperor, was for months a ghost town.

In the end the British won because the Mutiny was confined to the sepoys recruited in Oudh, and the British had access to adequate alternative recruiting territories. The Sikhs of the Punjab, the Pathans, hitherto enemies of the British rule, and the Ghurkas, welcomed the chance to plunder the rich cities of Oudh in the basins of the Ganges and the Jamuna. These replacement Indian armies were composed of men who seem not to have feared the missionary talents of their new paymasters, and served through remarkable hardships with great zeal. The armies of the Bombay and Madras Presidencies recruited, unlike the Bengal army, from low-caste Hindus were largely unaffected, and in the end were happy to do battle with their mutinous co-religionists. It must not be forgotten that the Indian Mutiny was contained, if not defeated, by Indians prepared to die in a British cause. In addition the technological resources put at the disposal of the British by the Industrial Revolution proved, in the end, adequate to the strains, and large numbers of British soldiers could be rushed to India by steamship from China, Ceylon and Africa, from Britain and Australia. The existence of a small section of railway from Calcutta helped to hurry the British relief forces to the front.

Above all, as is clearly implied in Farrell's narrative, the Indian mutineers had more instigators than leaders. Tactical military advantages were rarely utilised with any strategic sense. The aims of the mutineers remained disjointed. Even where the Mutiny was successful, success seems to have bred immediate dissension, the Muslim Sepoys wishing to march to Delhi to join the Moghul Emperor, while the Hindus, having killed or driven away the Europeans, wanted to rally to a Hindu leader, or to return to their families and the villages from which they had been recruited. It took the British with their new Indian allies two years to subdue the last pockets of unrest, but after the spring of 1858 their operations increasingly had the air of a glorified foxhunt.

For the East India Company, the Mutiny was a mortal blow. The British Parliament at Westminster revoked the Company's licence to rule India. Rightly or wrongly, it was recognised that Britain ruled India by the sword; but that until such time as an alternative presented itself a British administration answerable, at least, to the British Parliament and people should attempt the task of government in India. The (in retrospect) amazingly rapid strides by which British India came within ninety years to independence and partition into Pakistan, India, Bangladesh, and Burma are beyond the scope of any study of Farrell's novel.

The characters in the novel

It might be said that Farrell's characters epitomise the reasons why the Bengal army mutinied and also why after the initial shocks the mutineers failed to overcome the apparently vulnerable, isolated British garrison.

The mutiny was, Farrell suggests, brought about by the crass materialism, the naively aggressive display of Christian faith and the uninformed paternalism of British India. Rarely in the novel is there any discussion with Indians about Indian circumstances; even the conversations that do take place, notably between Mr Willoughby and the *zemindars* (Chapter 6) or between Hari and George Fleury (Chapter 5) or later on in the novel between Hari and Mr Hopkins (Chapter 14), are all distinguished by the clear gulf of incomprehension that divided Briton from Indian, a gulf made worse by the ignorance and the discourtesy Farrell's Englishmen display towards any opinion coming from an Indian source. Perhaps Farrell overpaints the ignorance and indifference of the British, and the absence of contact between the races. For the reader of this historic novel must remember that Indians, even those who were not tainted with the contamination of having accepted conversion to Christianity like Ram, Fleury's friend during the siege, were prepared to die for the British, in what must have seemed in June, July and August 1857 a totally lost cause. Outside the frame of the novel Indians of all castes and faiths were happy to be recruited into the British service to put down the rebellion of their co-religionists. It is not an adequate explanation to put this down simply to the attractions of regular pay. Indians then as now, and even in the novel, showed their clear ability to rise above the purely materialistic attractions of the world.

Within the novel, Farrell draws our attention to the cohesiveness of the British community. Although the ladies quarrel and intrigue, and are uncharitable to anyone who has lost her virtue, like Lucy Hughes, or who happens to have lice in her hair, and although the men of the garrison differ on tactics, and even, like Mr Rayne, exploit temporary positions of power for personal gain, nonetheless the community is one. Farrell finds the social cohesion of the British under attack a matter for ironic, not always sympathetic, treatment. The survival of the British and the few fit, armed, trained sepoy loyalist supporters, can only be achieved at the expense of driving out the Indian Christians (Chapter 8), although, we may presume, the Indian Christians would have received brutal treatment outside the Residency from the mutineers and their supporters eager to expunge all trace of the hated foreign religion from Indian soil. Mr Hampton makes his Sunday-school class of British children take a rare issue of sweetmeats to the unfortunate 'native' Christians still huddling close to the Residency's defences (Chapter 9). The unaccustomed food is rejected for fear of additional offence to unspoken taboo. Farrell mocks the self-centred inhumanity of the British and equally the apparently superstitious folly of the Indians.

For Farrell no one person or cause should be seen as wholly good, neither Indian nor British. He looks at the society he has discovered in mid-Victorian India, and invites us, his readers, to look at it through his eyes, but what he sees merits contempt more often than compassion. Mr Willoughby, the Magistrate, who at some points in the novel, as when he tries to get Indian *zemindars* to protect their lands against flooding, or when he instinctively recognises that Dr McNab is right in his scientific appraisal of the causes of and treatment for cholera, seems to be almost worthy of respect, is shown to be in the end to be a sham, a man obsessed with the absurdities of phrenology and contemptuous of his fellow men.

Dr McNab is presented to us as a man of some intelligence and humanity: in face of insult, he tries twice to save the life of his persecutor Dr Dunstaple, but Farrell keeps him in the background; we are not permitted to see into his thoughts about the siege of the society in which he finds himself. George Fleury is introduced to us as a young romantic, a poet, an intellectual, a person of feeling. But he is soon shown to be shallow, foolish, naive to a degree, insensitive to the feelings of Hari. Abruptly, from being for the first third of the novel the character on whom Farrell has focused most attention, he is relegated to the background from which he emerges with an absurd new invention of a weapon of destruction; or at the end of the book, squalidly, on his way to visit a prostitute. Only Mr Hopkins somehow survives the corrosive acid of Farrell's plan. Mr Hopkins begins badly. He is a harsh, remote father; he is foolish, even in the wisdom of his insight into the likelihood of impending troubles as he wanders around Calcutta trying to stir up official interest in the warning signals he has noticed. He seems a weak tool for unintelligent application of the materialist precepts of mid-Victorian Britain to an unwilling and unprepared India. Moreover, he makes mistakes. When trouble is certain he orders the destruction of a mosque that is in the likely field of fire from the Residency, but he overlooks the fact that the simple mud-walled hovels around the mosque will afford better cover for the mutineers' snipers and artillery. But gradually he emerges as a hero, of a risible kind. His true worth is revealed as the siege progresses, as the tribulations and the probability of ultimate catastrophe grow, and as everyone else except Dr McNab falls away, unequal to the strains of decision-making and of maintaining the morale of the starving, diseased and outnumbered garrison. The dross flakes away from his spirit, as the ramparts and the buildings of his pathetic fortress gradually collapse under the onslaught of gunfire and the monsoon rains. He abandons his faith in progress. He understands the worthlessness of the notion that the British enjoy divine approval and have a manifest destiny to force India to accept a modernisation scheme that depends on materialist fancies and inventions which ultimately are only to be measured by their effectiveness in dealing out death and destruction. By self-discipline, and a simple sense of duty, he nurses himself with some help from Miriam Lang (for whom he may, or may not, harbour amorous longings) through the convalescent stages of erysipelas and then more seriously, through a nervous breakdown. He recovers in time to purge the reduced garrison of the demoralisation brought about by Mr Rayne's black-marketeering and Mr Willoughby's weakness, and to bring the garrison through the last desperate stage of the defence to survival.

But the effort, Farrell suggests, has taken everything from the Collector except his life. Mr Hopkins is at the end simply an empty shell, an agnostic. Indifferent to his family and the opportunities of creative benevolence made possible by his wealth and the reputation won by his conduct of the siege, he spends his retirement in brooding withdrawal at his London club. Farrell could not be accused of finding inspiration for an optimistic view of man's state in his historic interpretation.

Part 4

Hints for study

How to improve your understanding of
The Siege of Krishnapur

(1) As with all examination set-texts, the only certain and satisfactory way to an examiner's heart is through an adequate, detailed knowledge and understanding of the text and of the context. You must read and re-read the book. The Penguin edition is clearly printed, and although the novel is relatively long, the plot is fairly easy to follow. None of the characters is investigated with any great depth or subtlety. None of the situations is complex, although the design of George Fleury's new weapon of war, the Cavalry Eradicator, requires some thought. The arguments between for example, Dr Dunstaple and Dr McNab over the causes of and the cure for cholera, would have been clear to laymen, even if the Magistrate, Mr Willoughby, had not been there to underline for us where truth and wisdom lie. Similarly, it is not difficult for a non-Christian to follow the arguments with which the Church of England Padre (priest) attempts to re-establish George Fleury's faith on the basis of an absolutely literal interpretation of the Holy Bible. The most intricate part of the plot is the unravelling of the role played at each successive stage in the book by the Collector, Mr Hopkins.

(2) If you can remember a characteristic or striking quotation with which to give colour to a character or a situation, so much the better. For example, when the Collector, on whom all responsibility rests, is lapsing into delirium from the effects of the sickness erysipelas, Pain, capitalised, is a 'round, red, throbbing presence', sitting beside, but clearly outside, Mr Hopkins.

In the open controversy before the assembled garrison over the treatment for cholera, the fact that all the besieged began to take sides and to declare their allegiance by carrying cards reading: 'In case of cholera please carry the bearer of this card to . . . [the favoured doctor of the moment]', the name possibly being changed several times as the arguments raged to and fro, is a striking image, and well worth mentioning at any relevant point.

Do not worry too much if you cannot recall the precise words of a quotation or description. Never attempt to carry into the examination room a long quotation in your head. A reasonably approximate version, showing that you have read and understood the work, will be rewarded with the examiner's favour. The important things are to remember, and to spell correctly, the characters' names; to remember the status of each within the novel, and the role each plays as the novel evolves; and to remember the basic outline of the plot.

The novel is meant to stand by itself, and be self-sufficient, and self-explanatory. It is a fictional interpretation of a historic tragedy. It shows how a group of Britons at the height of British imperial power might react to a sudden reversal of fortune and endure, or succumb to, a siege. Farrell did, as he acknowledges in the postscript to the novel, take much of his inspiration from real events, and the diaries and narrative accounts of men and women who had to endure in the course of the Indian Mutiny just such ordeals as those described by Farrell.

It would help your understanding if you could spare the time to read one of the shorter standard histories of the British in India in the nineteenth century, written by either Indian or British historians. The least expensive, and by no means the worst, is Volume 2 of the Penguin *History of India* written by T.G.P. Spear. The short, thorough and interesting work, *A Short History of India*, by W.H. Moreland, and Sir A.C. Chatterjee is still available, having been reprinted often by Longman (Orient Longman). Remember that Farrell is making a comment on historical reality.

(3) Bearing in mind that Farrell is trying to set his novel in an accurate historical setting, to heighten the impact on his mainly British readers, you will find it rewarding to try to imagine how you would organise the defences of a civilian residence with outbuildings, if you had Mr Hopkins's experience, technical resources and his premonitions of disaster to come. Ask yourself how you would cope with the basic phenomena of human panic, overcrowding, disease, the promiscuous mixing of races and social classes, men, women and children, to say nothing of the military perils. How would you stock up for a siege on the assumption that you have no electricity, your outside water supplies fail, and you have to solve major problems of sanitation disposal, cooking, and of keeping the disposal of the dead both ethically decent and sanitary? How would you keep horses fed and active for cavalry action after two months of deprivation?

(4) Make a checklist of the major characters in the book. Without referring to the text write down your own appraisal of their strengths and weaknesses. How do they behave to each other? How clearly do they reveal their inner qualities of character, their upbringing, their training, and their sense of responsibility to each other and their general situation?

Extracts appropriate to particular topics

These extracts are meant to help you to deal with two main themes, the British in India and the evolution of the character of Mr Hopkins, the Collector.

The British position in India in 1857: Chapter 1: Mr Hopkins feels safe in the Krishnapur Residency; Chapter 2: British social life in Calcutta; Chapter 3: British social life in Krishnapur; Chapter 4: the British Community at Krishnapur divided into the 'croakers' and the 'confident'; Chapter 6: the Collector and Mr Willoughby debate defensive positions and witness the first signs of the mutiny at Krishnapur.

The Collector at the height of his powers preparing for the siege: Chapter 1: the first discovery of 'chapatis'; the Collector is alarmed and begins to plan for a possible uprising and the defence of the Residency; the Collector's sympathy with the arts and his compassion for women; Chapter 2: concern for his wife; the Collector tries to warn the British Government in Calcutta of impending crisis; ridicule is poured on his 'alarmist rumours'; Chapter 3: the fruits of the Great Exhibition; belief in Christianity and the material triumphs of Western industry; Chapter 4: discussion with Dr McNab about his preparations against attack and his relations with his children; debates with General Jackson on the need for preparation; Chapter 5: discusses impact of Christianity with Miriam Lang; Chapter 7: the Collector takes military command of the Residency; first burning of Europeans' houses in Krishnapur; plans for defence; should the mosque be destroyed?; Chapter 8: Indian Christians driven out of the Residency; Chapter 9: the Collector's dinner party, at which Vokins announces the firing of the bungalows, one by one, by the mutineers; the Collector recalls a conversation about model workers' houses; explains the incarceration of Hari.

The Collector during the siege: Chapter 11: the Collector's first major problems; the Collector and the garrison pets; his selective charity to the world's poor; he conquers fear; Chapter 13: coping with daughters and womankind in general; the Collector debates the Indian rejection of superior culture; visits the hospital; Chapter 14: supervises the detail of the defences; revels in the triumph of statistical science as applied to human society; debates phrenology with Hari; embraces Mrs Lang and drinks tea with the subalterns. The stresses show; at Fleury's birthday party he has a moment of happiness; Chapter 17: he avoids controversy with Mr Hampton; his shell-shattered bedroom as a reflection of his state of mind; Chapter 18: Hari released; Chapter 19: the Collector collapses with erysipelas; Chapter 20: is nursed through delirium by

Miriam; Chapter 21: loses faith in the British mission in India, but recovers from erysipelas; Chapter 23: recovery, marked by his undertaking his own laundry; rebukes the women for malice; Chapter 24: tries to set an example by rebuilding rain-eroded ramparts himself; his file is useful for making chain-shot; Chapter 25: nervous breakdown; Chapter 26: his sense of duty reasserts itself; he overthrows Mr Rayne's black market; adjudicates reluctantly between the quarrelling doctors; Chapter 27: food and ammunition running out; Chapter 29: the Collector shapes fresh plans for defences and last-ditch actions; Chapter 30: in desperate action; he revises his once high opinion of the Great Exhibition, and allows himself 'contempt for the greedy merchants of England,'; is pestered by the Padre, just as the garrison is relieved; Chapter 32: disillusionment of Mr Hopkins.

Answering questions on the novel

1. Have the question clearly in your mind as you write your answer paragraph by paragraph. Nothing loses marks so quickly as irrelevance. Make sure you understand the full significance of each question before writing anything.
2. After you have thought about the question, try to take a few moments to plan your reply. Make two columns on a sheet for rough working, and jot down in one column your main themes; in the other the illustrations you will use for each theme.
3. While detailed quotations are not essential, if you can quote verbatim so much the better. A short significant phrase will suffice; and a close approximation is better than no effort at all. A good examiner will be looking for points to reward, however small.
4. Do not quote from irrelevant authorities. The examiner, who has probably read all the critics, wants to read your views, and will reward your originality so long as it is relevant to the questions. Never be afraid to express your own opinion. Luckily Farrell has not attracted the vampire hordes of the English literary critics.
5. Check your spelling, your punctuation and the shaping of your paragraphs. Make your sentences short. Avoid parentheses. Make sure your paragraphs consist of *groups* of sentences, not single sentences, and are genuine units of sense.

Plan for sample answers to questions

(1) '*The Siege of Krishnapur* is essentially a story of disillusionment and of the loss of innocence.' Do you agree with this comment? Do you find the characters reveal more ignorance than innocence? In

attempting this part of the question, make it clear how you differentiate between ignorance and innocence.

Answering the question: The question is, like all examination questions, a gentle trap. Before answering any question allow yourself a few moments for thought about how to avoid the trap, which in this case is to embark on an answer without realising that the question has several parts, and that innocence, ignorance and disillusionment need careful definition in your own mind before you shape your reply. It is simpler, you may think, to agree with the proposition than to disagree, given the plot offered by Farrell.

Developing your argument: There are shades of difference between each of the concepts in the question. So long as you state clearly your own interpretation of the differences, you will be able to see that certain characters in the book do behave like people ignorant, innocent, or disillusioned, and thus you will be able to give examples in your answer. In your opening you can be straightforward, indicating your agreement with the basic propositions and perhaps offering the examiner your interpretation of the three states of mind. You might wish to suggest that ignorance implies the failure or reluctance to learn from evidence which is available; and that the novel opens by portraying ignorance on a grand scale. The ruling British society in India is remarkably ignorant of the India over which it rules, and as a result is unfeeling about religious taboos and indifferent to the cultural sensitivities of the Hindu and Muslim communities of India. The British despise the land they temporarily reside in, because they do not care to learn.

Innocence, on the other hand, might be taken as indicating that knowledge is lacking through inexperience, in the absence of any of the destructive emotions like greed, pride or lust. You might wish to suggest that Harry Dunstaple and George Fleury have an innocent approach to life in their relationships with, say, the Indians or with women. They mean no harm. Be careful: Fleury, especially, is both ignorant and innocent.

Disillusionment, finally, you might say indicates a state of mind following the realisation that the beliefs, even the knowledge, that we have acquired through experience, learning or thought, turn out to be either worthless or erroneous. The Collector is not ignorant of India and of the poverty-stricken condition of the Indians. At the beginning of the Mutiny, he believes in progress, and the improvement of the condition of man by the application of science, technology and the products of Western industry to the problems of India. His disillusionment stems from his realisation that he has misunderstood both the nature and the extent of the problems of India, and overestimated the ease with which Western technology can be applied in India, except, that is, for weapons of mutual destruction. He has also, it is clear, a certain faith in human nature which in large part is based on ignorance. As he acquires knowledge of human frailty, of the greed and selfishness of many of the garrison, and of the lack of charity among the womenfolk, he grows tired. You may wish to stress that his breakdown stems from his being made aware of human frailty. When he was the Collector he was too remote from the human problems of the people over whom he ruled. Now, in the besieged garrison, he is personally involved directly with the personal problems of command; and proximity, he finds, is wearing and dispiriting.

He had believed that the more the human soul is tested under stress, the higher will it rise; but now in the siege he learns to his disgust that the human soul, even of the educated man, is weak, and deeply flawed, and affords us no opportunity for optimism.

Other points: You might care to stress that both ignorance and innocence are exemplified in the attitudes of George Fleury and of Harry Dunstaple to women. George is shown as ignorant of ordeal by flirtation in the picnic expedition to the Botanic Gardens at Alipore (Chapter 2). Harry and George are so ignorant of the female body (and presumably of the facts of life) that they can in all innocence and with no lustful intent scrape down the body of Lucy Hughes when she has the misfortune to be the victim of the massive swarms of cockchafers, and find to their amazement that she has pubic hair (Chapter 22).

You might care to exemplify the differences between ignorance and innocence from the quarrels between Dr Dunstaple and Dr McNab (especially in Chapters 25 and 26). Dr Dunstaple is clearly meant to personify an outdated unscientific approach to medicine. His ignorance is based on prejudice, and on arguments which even a layman such as the Magistrate, Mr Willoughby, can see are based on fallacies, and on his hatred for Dr McNab. The latter on the other hand is clearly innocent of malice, is totally devoted to the vindication of the best scientific approach to medicine, and tries time and again to save Dr Dunstaple's life.

Finally, you could perhaps underline your knowledge and understanding of the novel by emphasising, by way of contrast, that in spite of the general atmosphere of disillusionment, the character that emerges best from the novel is that of Dr McNab, whose determination to acquire medical knowledge through study and the utilisation of scientific facts fortifies his spirit against adversity and qualifies him for Mr Hopkin's memorial: 'He was the best of us all.'

One trick to remember: do re-read the question at the beginning of each paragraph of your reply to help to ensure that the lines of your argument are relevant.

(2) 'The overthrow of a noble soul': is this a fair description of Mr Hopkins's role in the novel?

Suggested line of argument: After the mandatory pause to think about the question, you might do worse than establish that in spite of many failings, the Collector indeed does have the soul of a leader of men, of a man whose character is marked by a certain nobility. Once you have established your case, the answer can, with care, be based on simple narrative.

The factors which might illuminate your reply include Mr Hopkins's intelligent interpretation of the meaning of the circulating 'chapatis', and his efforts (unavailing as it turns out) to warn the British government in Calcutta of the possibility of trouble; and the courage with which he faces ridicule in insisting on having a defensive earthwork built round the Residency and the adjacent houses and buildings. You might also allude to the responsibility with which the Collector faces up to the unwelcome duties as military commander thrust upon him by the exigencies of the siege and the absence of competent military alternatives.

Make it clear in your opening that you recall that the Collector is human, and fallible. He is a family man, but he has forgotten—or wilfully omitted—to make a will. He is an overbearing, almost cruel father. His daughters are terrified of him. His attitude to women is typical of men—even of intellectual men—of his time. He sees women in the Residency as weak and silly, and deduces that their fragility and silliness stem from their intrinsic nature, not from their conditioning.

The Collector, you should point out, has to undertake the moral and military leadership of the beleaguered garrison when the hapless old General Jackson is mortally wounded during the mutiny at Captainganj. You might describe in as much detail as you recall the Collector's belief that the Christian God he worships reveals Himself both in the fact that the British rule India, and in the superiority of the British culture, revealed to the world in the British manufactures at the Great Exhibition of 1851. This belief in British superiority gives him at first the moral strength he needs to guide the trapped Residency garrison through the early weeks of the siege. He is at first the very model of self-reliance, a self-tutored organiser of resistance.

You could trace the decline of the Collector's self-reliance from his unfortunate attack of erysipelas; although he recovers sufficiently to resume leadership of the garrison, husbanding the scanty resources wisely, working out planned withdrawal after withdrawal to ever smaller perimeters as the numbers of defenders diminish, you can see that the ordeal in many ways saps and erodes his philanthropy. He is depressed by human inadequacies, and by the moral and physical squalor around him, and his equilibrium is overthrown by the weight of decision-making thrust upon him by the rest of the garrison. They, with the exception of Dr McNab, reveal themselves as empty cynics like Mr Willoughby, unfit for command, as greedy profiteers like Mr Rayne, or as ignoble mortals obsessed with imagined wrongs, like Dr Dunstaple or Mr Hampton, the padre. In the end it is young, thoughtless Harry Dunstaple who accidentally causes the Collector's collapse by thrusting upon Mr Hopkins the decision about firing grapeshot to clear the monsoon-fed undergrowth that threatens to cover the mutineers' attack.

Again the Collector, by an effort of will which proves his sterling character, recovers and leads the garrison to survival. But he has clearly been drained not merely of physical energy but of all idealism. He no longer believes in British scientific progress; he can no longer identify his Christian God with any heaven-sent mission to lead India to material improvement and enrichment. In the end he leaves India for retirement as a moral husk, without religious faith or confidence in the materialist civilisation of Britain, as epitomised in the much vaunted Great Exhibition.

Specimen questions

1. What do you understand as J.G. Farrell's main purpose in writing a book set in India in the year 1857?
2. Analyse the state of British society in India before and after the Mutiny, illustrating your answer from J.G. Farrell's descriptions of the British in Calcutta and Krishnapur.
3. Why does Farrell find the circumstances of a siege to be appropriate to his purposes? Trace the evolution of the plot, and of the characters, from what you recall of the events seen through the eyes of Mr Hopkins or of George Fleury.
4. 'Farrell does not provide satisfactorily consistent characters.' Discuss, with reference to the sequence of events, the characterisation in *The Siege of Krishnapur*.
5. 'The wonder is that the British should have thought it worth their while trying to stay in India.' Discuss, and illustrate by reference to the problems the British exiles faced in ordinary and in extra-ordinary times, as shown in the novel
6. Who is the real hero of *The Siege of Krishnapur*? Is there a hero? If so, what makes him heroic?
7. 'J.G. Farrell finds it difficult to understand what motivates a woman. Hence his female characters are only shadowy pegs on which to hang the affections of his male characters.' Discuss with reference to Miriam Lang, Lucy Hughes and Louise Dunstaple.

8. 'Farrell's novel *The Siege of Krishnapur*, fails because it misses the chance to explore adequately the tensions that existed between the Indians and the British.' Discuss. Do you think that a better balance would have been given by giving us a wider point of view? Are the British self-critical? How does their belief, that their presence in India is justified, manifest itself?

9. If you had been asked to help J.G. Farrell to write his book and to provide a commentary from an Indian viewpoint, what kind of character would you have created? Where would he or she have been throughout the siege? And what would finally have happened to make your character consistent with J.G. Farrell's plot? You may use one of the Indian characters that do feature in the novel, or invent a new character, either within the garrison or on the side of the mutineers.

10. 'The British rule over India was destroyed by Christianity, or at least by the activities of clergymen.' Discuss and illustrate from the conversations of the Padre and Father O'Hara with each other and with any other characters.

11. 'Farrell is better at describing actions than in chronicling states of mind and philosophic debates.' Is this a fair summary of Farrell's talents, as revealed in *The Siege of Krishnapur*? Whichever point of view you endorse, illustrate your answer with references to the novel.

12. 'Farrell's two medical doctors represent the extremes of Victorian medicine: Dunstaple is ignorance and bigotry incarnate, while McNab is the true scientist, humble, intelligent and forever questioning'. Is this fair? Illustrate your reply with as many references to the novel as you can manage.

13. 'The Collector, Mr Hopkins, gradually emerges as a natural leader, the right man in the right place at the right time.' Trace the evolution of Mr Hopkin's character.

14. 'Farrell is a master of the innuendo.' Do you agree that you have understood more of J.G. Farrell's purposes from what is not explored in detail, but only hinted at? Illustrate Farrell's talent for the indirect exposition.

15. Do you think that Farrell has written a true historical novel?

16. '*The Siege of Krishnapur* is as anti-Indian as it is anti-British.' Discuss.

17. 'The absence of children from the detailed characterisation is a major flaw in *The Siege*.' Discuss. What do you think would have been the main problems of survival for an intelligent but untrained child trapped in the Residency?

18. How does Farrell reveal the innocence, and the coming to maturity, of Harry Dunstaple and George Fleury?

19. How effective have you found Farrell's technique of story-telling, and his style and use of language in keeping you interested in the novel? What have you noticed about his language and style?
20. Where do the author's sympathies lie? How does Farrell reveal his commitment for or against a character at any point? Would you say he looks at events through his characters' eyes, or from a neutral standpoint? Is his use of irony an indication of contempt for a character?
21. '*The Siege of Krishnapur* was written to be made into a film, not to survive as a novel in a library.' If you were a film producer, what visual effect would you concentrate upon?
22. Do you think that *The Siege of Krishnapur* will still be read in fifty years' time? If you do, why?
23. Discuss Farrell's treatment of sexual relationships.
24. 'Farrell treats the sufferings of the garrison as essentially comic.' Do you find Farrell funny? How can humour help to make you aware of tragedy?

Part 5

Suggestions for further reading

The text

FARRELL, J.G.: *The Siege of Krishnapur*, Weidenfeld and Nicolson, London, 1973.
FARRELL, J.G.: *The Siege of Krishnapur*, Penguin Books, Harmondsworth, 1975, 1979, 1980 (twice), 1982.

Other works by J.G. Farrell

A Man From Elsewhere, Hutchinson, London, 1963.
The Lung, Hutchinson, London, 1965.
A Girl in the Head, Cape, London, 1967. (Reprinted by Fontana, London, 1978.)
Troubles, Cape, London, 1970. (Reprinted by Penguin Books, Harmondsworth, 1979.)
The Singapore Grip, Weidenfeld and Nicolson, London, 1978. (Reprinted by Fontana, London, 1980.)
The Hill Station, Weidenfeld and Nicolson, London, 1981. (Reprinted by Fontana, London 1982.)

Books on the Indian Mutiny

A great many books have been written about the Indian Mutiny. One of the best, and particularly relevant to Farrell since it contains very interesting descriptions of life in besieged Lucknow, is:

COLLIER, R.: *The Sound of Fury*, Collins, London, 1963. Contains an extensive bibliography indicating a life-time of study.

The classic, detailed nineteenth-century descriptions of the Mutiny are still gripping, and well worth studying if you can find them in a second-hand bookshop or public library:
HOLMES, T.R.: *A History of the Indian Mutiny*, 5th ed., Macmillan, London, 1898. Perhaps the most balanced of the Victorian interpretations.

RUSSELL, W.H.: *My Diary in India*, Routledge, London, 1860. A fair newspaper reporter's view.

KAYE, SIR J.W. and MALLESON, COL. G.B.: *History of the Indian Mutiny*, 6 vols, Longman, London, 1897. Enormous and vivid, but needs to be read with care, since it is committed to the rightness of the British cause. Nevertheless it pulls few punches over the excesses on the British as well as the Indian side.

For the modern Indian view, see:

MAJUMDAR, R.C.: *The Sepoy Mutiny and the Revolt of 1857*, 2nd ed., rev., K.L. Mukhopadhya, Calcutta, 1963. There are extensive (and by no means overlapping) bibliographies in both these works.

SEN, S.N.: *Eighteen Fifty-Seven*, Government of India, New Delhi, 1957.

To see the Indian Mutiny in the wider context of Indian history and of the relations between the British and the Indians, you should read one of the many excellent general histories. Among the best are:

HUNTER, SIR W.W.: *A History of British India*, 2 vols, Longman, London, 1899. Reissued in several Indian editions since, and still available in libraries.

MORELAND, W.H. and CHATTERJEE, SIR A.C.: *A Short History of India,* Longman, London and Calcutta, 1944 (and subsequent editions).

SPEAR, SIR P.: *A History of India*, 2 vols, Pelican, Penguin Books, Harmondsworth, 1956 (and subsequent editions).

Studies of J.G. Farrell's writings

So far there has been little academic assessment of Farrell's quality. Perhaps the most interesting comments on his life and work are contained in the essays written by John Spurlin, Margaret Drabble and Malcolm Dean, and appended to his unfinished novel, *The Hill Station*, Fontana, London, 1982.

Other novels about the British in India

The Mutiny has inspired many authors. Among the more readable, those that bear comparison with *The Siege of Krishnapur* include:

KAYE, M.M.: *Shadow of the Moon*, Longman, London, 1957. (Reprinted by Corgi Books, London, 1971 and subsequently.)

MASTERS, J.: *Nightrunners of Bengal*, Michael Joseph, London, 1951. (Reprinted by Penguin Books, Harmondsworth, 1955 and subsequently.)

STEEL, F.A.: *On the Face of the Waters*, Heinemann, London, 1896.

Mrs Steel married a senior member of the Indian Civil Service and lived for many years in India. This novel, still exciting today, is based on personal accounts of first-hand experience.

After the Mutiny had been quelled, neither side found it possible to forget—nor, one suspects, to understand—what had gone wrong. Among the British, the Mutiny remains a subject for constant, neurotic wound-scratching. Certainly the British community in India became even more isolated from the Indians. Cantonments, houses, banks and railway stations were designed for quick conversion to defensive bastions that could withstand a sudden outbreak of violence. For an understanding of the British community in its aloof remoteness and its convictions of moral rectitude, see:

FORSTER, E.M.: *A Passage to India*, Arnold, London 1924.

For fictional attempts to show teachers or missionaries bridging the gap between the communities, see:

THOMPSON, E.: *An India Day*, Knopf, London, 1927.
THOMPSON, E.: *Night Falls on Siva's Hills*, Heinemann, London, 1929.
THOMPSON, E.: *A Farewell to India*, Macmillan, London, 1933.

The author of these notes

JOHN RIDDY is a senior administrator at the University of Stirling, Scotland, and has taught courses in South Asian literature for the English Department there. He graduated in history from Oxford, where he later did research on Indian history after having worked in India for some years. He has been a university administrator at Oxford and Ahmadu Bello University, Nigeria, and has published essays on various aspects of the history of nineteenth-century India. He is married with three awful children.